HOLLYWOOD HUSSEIN

How the U.S. Really Captured Saddam

By
Ken Baker

Verona Publishing, Inc.
P.O. Box 24071
Edina, Minnesota 55424

www.veronapublishing.com

Verona Publishing is pleased to present HOLLYWOOD HUSSEIN How the U.S. Really Captured Saddam By KEN BAKER. If you are interested in purchasing more copies or if you are interested in books on other topics books can be ordered at www.veronapublishing.com
When ordering in bulk email us the type and number of books required at info@veronapublishing.com

See our other titles and at www.veronapublishing.com or wherever books are sold.

For questions or comments, contact us at info@veronapublishing.com

Cover art by Robert Delgadillo

Design and layout by Barbara Keith.

Technical Consulting by Tim Yearneau

HOLLYWOOD HUSSEIN How the U.S. Really Captured Saddam 2005

Published by Verona Publishing, Inc., P.O. Box 24071, Edina, Minnesota 55424

 Printed in the United States of America.

Library of Congress Cataloging-in-Publication Data:

Library of Congress Control Number: 2005926384

ISBN 0-9667037-9-0

Verona Publishing, Inc.
P.O. Box 24071
Edina, Minnesota 55424

www.veronapublishing.com

ACKNOWLEDGEMENTS

Sweet thanks goes out to my family, who tolerated the creative mania behind this book that stole me from them for weekends at a time. Dada loves you.

The dedication, energy and commitment of my talented *Us Weekly* teammates is a daily inspiration, and I love you all.

Peace out to Scott Cosman of Flynet Pictures who gave me the skinny on the paparazzi.

Thanks to Monty Wilson of Verona Publishing for having the genius to see this project's potential, and to publicity guru Michael Wright for his enthusiastic promotion.

I am eternally grateful to former ABC News executive Dean Norland for taking a chance on a dumb jock back in 1992, and to Janice Min, Jann Wenner and Kent Brownridge for their generous support over the years.

Joyce Maynard, an expert novelist and dear friend, was the first person to tell me I could write fiction. Blame her for this.

John E. Friberg Jr. gave me spooky insights that I most definitely appreciate.

Thanks to all the friends who have lifted me up when I was down. I am always here for you.

I salute all the American soldiers who are fulfilling their patriotic duty, especially those who do it despite disagreeing with the reason they've been sent to fight.

Here's a shout-out to my boy George W. Bush and his posse for their endless supply of comic relief.

This author's message to those who thought this book was "too risky" to publish in the current political climate: You were wrong.

God bless America.

Ken Baker is the West Coast Executive Editor of *Us Weekly* and the author of two critically-acclaimed memoirs, "*Man Made: A Memoir of My Body*" and "*They Don't Play Hockey in Heaven: A Dream, a Team and My Comeback Season*", which chronicled his experience as a professional hockey goalie. Baker, who holds a master's degree from the Columbia University Graduate School of Journalism, has worked in the Washington, D.C., bureau of ABC News and as a staff correspondent for *People* magazine. He lives in—where else?—Hollywood. For more information go to www.kenbaker.net.

CAST OF MAIN CHARACTERS
HOLLYWOOD HUSSEIN

Tom Peppers	*Them! Weekly* Hollywood Bureau Chief and in lust with London Marriott
The Paparazzi	The Eyes of America
Barry Posner	Special Assistant to the President and jealous of Tom Peppers
George W. Bush	President of the United States and "in charge"
Condoleezza Rice	National Security Adviser and better looking in person
Dick Cheney	Vice President and heart patient
Donald Rumsfeld	Secretary of Defense and bespectacled
Colin Powell	Secretary of State and Cheney hater
Arnold Schwarzenegger	California governor/action hero
Mark Burton	Reality TV producer (*Survival, Who Wants To Be An American Hero*)
Ronald Stump	Business mogul and reality TV star
Jessica Peppers	Tom Peppers's hot wife
Bobby Lesser	*Them! Weekly* Editor-in-Chief
Ben Lay	CEO, Paliburton Inc.
London Marriott	Professional Celebrity
Saddam Hussein	The World's Worst Celebrity

Appearances are often deceiving.

—Aesop, *Fables*

Ken Baker is the West Coast Executive Editor of *Us Weekly* and the author of two critically-acclaimed memoirs, "*Man Made: A Memoir of My Body*" and "*They Don't Play Hockey in Heaven: A Dream, a Team and My Comeback Season*", which chronicled his experience as a professional hockey goalie. Baker, who holds a master's degree from the Columbia University Graduate School of Journalism, has worked in the Washington, D.C., bureau of ABC News and as a staff correspondent for *People* magazine. He lives in—where else?—Hollywood. For more information go to www.kenbaker.net.

Is the story you're about to read the truth? That's for you to decide. If my investigation taught me anything, it's that truth is merely the version of the facts we choose to believe.

Ken Baker
Hollywood, California

SUNDAY, DECEMBER 14, 2003

TIKRIT, Iraq (A.P.)—*Eight months after the fall of Baghdad, U.S. soldiers found and captured former Iraqi dictator Saddam Hussein in a hole in the ground late Saturday nine miles south of his hometown of Tikrit. Saddam was taken into custody without a single shot being fired. At a news conference in Baghad earlier today, coalition civil administrator L. Paul Bremer brought Iraqi journalists to their feet with shouts of joy when he announced, "Ladies and gentleman, we got him!"*

In a scene right out of a Hollywood movie, about 600 soldiers of the Army's 1st Brigade, 4th Infantry Division, and special operations forces of Task Force 121 conducted the raid in the farm in the village of Ad Dawr. Troops converged on a two-room mud hut that lay between two farmhouses. One room, which appeared to serve as a bedroom, was in disarray with clothes strewn about the area. The other room was a crude kitchen. Armed with a pistol, Saddam was found lying disoriented in 6-foot-deep hole equipped with a basic ventilation system. Military video released to the media shows a group of coalition soldiers patting each other on the back in celebration outside the compound.

U.S. officials said they had received "actionable intelligence" from someone close to Saddam's inner circle that he was hiding out at the location. The operation was dubbed "Red Dawn."

"It just takes finding the right person who will give you a good idea where he might be, and that's what happened," said Lt. Gen. Ricardo Sanchez, commander of U.S. forces in Iraq, who in recent weeks had received intelligence that narrowed the search to the Tikrit area. "The Iraqi people no longer need to fear a return of Saddam's tyranny," President George W. Bush said in a televised speech to the nation. "We should all be proud of the nation's military and intelligence professionals. Their dedication in bringing this brutal dictator to justice has led to today's victory for peace and democracy."

U.S. officials, citing classified informants, would not reveal the identities of the tipsters who led forces to Saddam's hideout other than to say it was three Americans inside Iraq who would receive the $25 million reward that had been offered to anyone with information leading directly to Saddam's capture.

GEORGE W. BUSH
President of the United States

In America, it's all about the big ideas. It's what makes America great, man. Well, that and Texas, of course.

Look, it doesn't take a rocket scientist to tell ya that America's always been a land of big ideas - not to mention a place that has, as those nasty little Dixie Chicks have said, wide open spaces. God, I love that Dixie Chicks tune. Don't agree with their politics, of course. But you gotta love 'em because we're all Americans, after all. We invented democracy, freedom, high-tech military stuff. Heck, we even invented television, didn't we? Important stuff—that's America, pal. My secret plan to get Saddam fell into the category of big freakin' important stuff. Saddam simply had to be brought to justice. End of story. Until that evil Iraqi dictator was captured, our job—and the job of the Coalition of the Willing—would not have been apprehended fully. Plus, hey, my daddy would be proud of his boy! YouknowwhatImean?

It's no different than when I ran my ball team, the Texas Rangers. If a player wasn't doin' his job, I damn well made sure we replaced him with a guy who could. And the same rules applied to our War on Terror: If the guys trackin' down Saddam couldn't find him, then I reckoned we just had to go and hire fellas who could. Heck, I did-n't care what those *beltway insiders* would say. They're probably readin' this book and rollin' their eyes right now, but I don't care. At least I stand for somethin'! I mean, ain't it better to stand for something sketchy and ill-thought than to stand for nothing at all? Anyway, I'm not sayin' the ends justifies the means, but in this case the means justified the ends. What I'm trying to say is to hell with them and their plans and paperwork and *policy*. You either buck the system or you're gonna get bucked. Or, as Daddy always likes to say, "Shit or get off the pot." So when Laura showed me that photo of Jenna in *Them! Weekly* it was like fireworks goin' off in my head. Sure, at first I was peeved, seein' that photo of my little Jenna trampin' around like some hussy in *Girls Gone Wild.* I sure know about phases, youthful *indiscretions.* Been there, done that. Ask my Daddy! I gave him more headaches than Dan

Quayle did when he gave speeches without a prompter. You know, I spent most of my time in the Texas Air National Guard doing what I like to call the three N's: dart playin', beer drinkin' and skirt chasin'.

But I've moved on, and God bless us that we can do that in America, the greatest country of all four the world's hemispheres. We can make mistakes and then pretend they never happened when it suits our self interest at a later date. It's the American way.

But back to that photo of Jenna in Them! .I remember Laura askin' me, "How'd they get that picture, W?" I told her the truth. "They found her, waited for the right moment, and bingo. They got her fair and square, honey." What do they call 'em? The paparotzy? Whatever you call 'em, those guys are just impressive, I have to say. For years, we had kept the press off Jenna by using a team of Jenna decoys. We'd done our best to throw them off, to distract them. Whenever Jenna got two sheets to the wind at some Austin drinkin' hole, I'd instructed the Secret Service guys to get her the hell out of Dodge before things got too ugly.

See, I understand the youth of America, and the things they do. I watch *American Idol.* Voted for Clay, rooted for Rueben. I done saw Britney Spears in concert at the Alamo Dome. That gal's somethin' else! Anyway, when Jenna flew down to Cancun with her friends for a vacation, we even had four different planes take off to different destinations, just to throw the media off her. Despite our best strategery, those darn Them! photographers not only found her, they got her. Like I said, impressive work. American ingenuity at work. So then Laura says to me, "If they could find Jenna I bet that darn magazine could find Saddam Hussein."

Laura can be a little slow on the uptake, ifyouknowwhatImean. That's why she didn't realize what she had just said. But that gal's comment had just given me here one of the greatest ideas of his administration. She's a good wife, that Laura. Y'all probably think she's a boring librarian with a bad hairdo, but I promise ya that she's a helluva a lot more than that. She's dumb like a dog. Or however the sayin'.

Daddy always says it doesn't matter where an idea comes from; what matters most is that it's a good one. And let me tell ya another thing: If I've learned anything in Washington over the last four years, it's that good ideas are hard to come by. So I knew I had to act with the surprise of a Mexican *bandito*! That's when I asked Condi and my friend Arnold to get that Operation Hollywood up and runnin'. It was a big idea, and the potential rewards were even bigger. It was a big thing. Texas big. America big.

PHONE CONVERSATION

GEORGE BUSH AND ARNOLD SCHWARZENEGGER

28 September 2003

2:33 p.m.

ARNOLD: It's so goot to hear from you, George Double-euuuuw.

BUSH: Same here. Congrats on everything, by the way. A real Republican victory to have you on the gubernatorial ticket out there. Your commander-in-chief salutes you!

ARNOLD: I'd say tanks for your help, but, George Double-euuuuw, you have done no tings to help my campaign out here.

BUSH: Sorry 'bout that, Arnie. That damn Karl Rove thought it was a bad idea—you know, to back someone like you who's soft on abortion, not to mention being a creature among the liberal Hollywood elite. I regret it and I ask for your forgiveness. But now that you've won the nomination I'll totally support you and should you win I will give California all the federal help you need to turn things around out there. Hope you understand.

ARNOLD: Honestly, I don't understand such tings. And that's why Ah-nuld is going to terminate you!

BUSH: But, but –

ARNOLD: Oh, just kitting, George Double-euuuuw. I was just pushing your presidential buttons. Let's get down to beezness. Why is such a busy man likeyou calling me out here? You know, I'm very busy right now with dis and dat, trying to do tings for the great state of Calee-fornia.

BUSH: Actually, Arnie, I'm callin' to ask a favor.

ARNOLD: Okay. Go for it. Make my day.

BUSH: You see, Arnie, I've got a little situation here on my hands, and I think the only way to fix it is, well, to give it the ole' Hollywood treatment.

ARNOLD: Well, you've come to the right guy. You know, I am Mr. Hollywood.

BUSH: Exactly. But lemme ask ya a question. Ever read *Them! Weekly* magazine?

ARNOLD: Of course. Maria and I have been in that magazine for different tings, usually in some paparazzi shots. They like to show me driving my Hummer and tings like dat. In fact, I have a copy right here in front of me.

(Bush hears a toilet flush.)

BUSH: Where are you? Did I catch ya at a bad time, partner?

ARNOLD: No, I am fine, just sitting on the shituh. Taking a gubernatorial crap! I do dat when I read dese magazines.

BUSH: Who's on the cover?

ARNOLD: It's that tasty London Marriott on the covuh. I could eat her like a strudel.

BUSH: Okay, good, that's the one I want you to read. Arnold, feast your eyes on page 32.

ARNOLD: Oh, let me see here ... yes! Ah-nuld loves dis section. Whatcha ma call it?

BUSH: Look-Alike of the Week.

ARNOLD: Dat's it. I sink that it's Maria's favorite section.

BUSH: Well, take a close look at it. Does that fella in the photo look familiar?

ARNOLD: Uh, I see a picture of some lazy homeless guy collecting cans on Venice Beach like a lazy freeloader. Welfare bum. He looks like dat worthless weakling Saddam Hussein. But dat picture is very funny to me. In fact, I used to pump iron on dat beach. I'd see lazy people like him all the time. Very funny to Ahnuld.

BUSH: Well, it ain't funny to me.

ARNOLD: How could you *not* sink dat's funny? Oh, you need to lighten up and not be such a girlie man. You career politicians need a better sense of humuh.

BUSH: Well, I'll tell you how it's not funny. But you have to promise not to tell anyone, especially not Maria. She'd have NBC tellin' the world about it before ya know it. Promise you can keep a secret?

ARNOLD: I promise.

BUSH: Pinky swear?

ARNOLD: Just shut up and tell Ahnuld!

BUSH: Okay. Well, that guy in the picture ain't no look-alike of Saddam Hussein.

ARNOLD: Then who is he?

BUSH: He's the real deal, Arnie.

ARNOLD: Say again, pleece. Ahnuld doesn't understand what you say to him.

BUSH: What I'm tryin' to say is that the dude in the picture is the real kahuna. That is the real Saddam Hussein!

ARNOLD: Are you trying to tell Ahnuld that Saddam Hussein has been living in the great state of Calee-fornia all dis time? That your military let him get away? That Saddam Hussein has been living right in my back yard?

BUSH: Yep. So much for homeland security, huh? Hehehehehe.

ARNOLD: You stupid idiot. You do have a situation on your hands. But, don't worry, George Double-euuuuw. Seriously, I sink I can help you with dis ting.

BUSH: Good, 'cause I done run out of ideas. But I had a feelin' you'd step up to the plate, for your country.

ARNOLD: Don't mention it. Just remember Calee-fornia when you roll out the pork barrel.

BUSH: Sure thing. I'll tell ya another thing: we're all lucky to have a true patriot, a true native son of America like you.

ARNOLD: Actually, I am not a native. I am from Austria.

BUSH: Oh, even better! That's where? ... Queens, right?

ARNOLD: No, Austria is a country in Europe.

BUSH: Gotcha! Just playin' with ya, Arnie. Hey, at the end of the day, all I ask is for your help on this little project.

ARNOLD: Well, today is your lucky day, because I know dis guy in Hollywood who can help you with your situation. His name is Mark Burton. He is a reality show producer. He is the best. I'll give you his numbuh.

BUSH: I owe ya one, pal.

ARNOLD: Yes, you do. Now Ahnuld has to terminate this conversation. *Hasta la vista* Georgie!

GEORGE W. BUSH

President of the United States

Okay, okay. Maybe I've been a bad Bushie. Maybe I was fibbin' with y'all about how I came to recruit those paparazzi. Told a little lie: It wasn't only Laura's idea to get the paparazzi for Operation Hollywood.

Arnold was the brains behind it. He helped me out puttin' me in touch with that genius Mark. But I swear on a stack of Bibles that everything else I'm tellin' ya is one-hundred-and-ten percent accurate and true. I swear. I wouldn't lie to ya 'bout that. If you can't trust Dubya, who can ya trust, right?

It probably ain't the most PC thing for a compassionate conservative such as myself to say, but I have nothin' against Hollywood folks. Actually, I love Hollywood! Sure, there are some bad apples out there. They got their chumps, their Michael Moores and Oliver Stones and Martin Sheens. But mosta Hollywood is filled with patriots who make good stuff.

Honestly, some of my fondest childhood memories came outta Hollywood. Mostly TV. There was *Gunsmoke* and *Bonanza*—now those were real American shows—with heroes, real rugged men of the West. I inspired to be like those fellas. Another of my favorite show was I *Dream of Jeannie*. Please don't tell Laura this—she hates it when I bullshit about women—but I used to get baked with my buddies watching that show, and we'd take a bong hit every time Barbara Eden said "master." Good times.

But Jeannie had an American theme, about the astronauts and whatnot. And I have Hollywood to thank for it. And I knew that if Mark Burton could get me out of the whole mess of finding Saddam on American soil, then I would have a lot more to thank Hollywood for than a hot chick in a bottle.

TOM PEPPERS

Hollywood Bureau Chief, *Them! Weekly*

A photographer who's a paparazzo is like a filmmaker who's a pornographer. Both get little respect from their straight colleagues, but they both make a lot of money. The most important thing they share, though, is the same artistic goal: the money shot. And I am the ultimate judge of the money shot. "It's Barry, on line one," my bored assistant suddenly droned over the intercom. Not knowing any Barries (except for Barry Williams from *The Brady Bunch*), I told my bored assistant to take a message, because, just a few minutes ago, a photographer had emailed me tabloid gold: J-pegs of Julia Roberts arguing with her husband. Or at least it looked like they were arguing. Honestly, though, it didn't matter. Fabloid Editor Rule #1: Never let the facts get in the way of a good picture.

What also made that Julia shot oh-so good was their chocolate Lab was pissing all over her two thousand-dollar snakeskin boots! It was a perfect modern-day paparazzi shot: a big star caught in an unglamorous moment, relegating her to mere civilian status. We had to lock it up—exclusively—before those weenies at People could get their greedy hands on it. Photos of this kind prove the point that my magazine tries to make every week: Stars are just like you. In fact, such a civilianizing shot can fetch up to a hundred grand a frame. These paparazzi—"paps," as they are known in the biz—hide in their SUV's behind tinted glass surviving on stale Doritos, bad coffee and the hunger for a money shot. They piss in coke cans, pop speed pills, and wait for that single moment to capture in time.

Celebrity magazine journalists like me rely on these voyeuristic paps more than ever, because, nowadays, the photo is king. It's become redundant to say celebrity magazines are "photo-driven." Long gone are the days of publicist-managed People profiles featuring a photo of the star boiling pasta in their kitchen or sitting on their porch petting their poodle. Readers nowadays want the dirt, the dish, the real story—not the one manufactured by the publicists. The American public is tired of phony-baloney Hollywood propaganda. They'd rather see Reese Witherspoon eating a jelly donut in a t-shirt than see her flashing her perfect smile in a Versace gown on the red carpet. The bottom line is that we live in an age of reality, not fantasy.

do you think ratings for the cable new networks went up after 9-11? Because there's nothing more real than life and death.

The public's appetite to know what the stars are really like has only increased since "reality" TV invaded our living rooms in the late 1990's. In the quaint, old days (say, back when I first became a celebrity journalist in 1995), more often than not we'd write celebrity profiles pegged to a "project," accompanied by posed shot. These days, though, if you first don't have a picture, then you usually don't have a story. And, in most cases, the picture is the story. A photo of Angelina Jolie kissing Brad Pitt conveys more information to readers than any words ever could.Back in 1998, a lot of geniuses out there predicted the end of the paparazzi era after that pack of French shooters chased Princess Diana to her death in a Paris tunnel. Then, in the aftermath of the September 11 attacks, more "experts" predicted the certain demise of our taste for escapist entertainment and celebrity obsession.

But just the opposite happened. In the post-Diana era, the celebrity-industrial complex has boomed. With every terrorist bombing, every Oval Office speech, every invasion of an Arab nation, the coverage of cheese-ball celebrities has only gotten more intense, and the number of journalists and photographers covering celebrities has increased more than ten-fold. Likewise, the tactics we employ to follow their every move have only gotten more aggressive, more invasive and more sophisticated. Forget baseball, my friends. Celebrity voyeurism has become our national pastime. I recently read a study finding that over the last year TV reporters said "Michael Jackson" thirteen times more often than they said "Saddam Hussein."

This new brand of hyper-journalism isn't practiced only by the five glossy celebrity news weeklies (*Us*, *People*, *Star*, *InTouch*, and, of course, *Them!*). If you turn on the tube you'll see the TV version of these celeb-centric magazines in the form of E! Entertainment Television (on which I appear regularly as an "expert") and the daily syndicated shows (Entertainment Tonight, Extra, Access Hollywood and Inside Edition). Because I appear on all of these shows to tattle on the latest celeb missteps I've become famous—a celebrity for talking about celebrities.

My journalism colleagues who work in the non-celebrity world could learn a thing or two from Hollywood journalists. The cable news channels made a big deal out of covering the war in Iraq with "embedded" reporters. What a joke! That's like me covering a movie based on a set visit supervised by a publicist. In these situations, where the powers-that-be have granted you access and bought your meals, it's implicit that you'll report favorably on them, and we usually do.

The same sort of biased coverage happens in straight journalism too. The result isn't the Truth, but rather such abominations as fawning stories about Tom Cruise's amazing martial arts skills and the U.S. Army's impressive GPS-guided armored divisions. Propaganda is propaganda. It's most effective when it's spread by the "media" rather than the beneficiary of the b.s.

The major cable news networks and daily newspapers are starting to use celebrity to draw the attention of their respective audiences. I recently sat on a panel at USC's journalism school. The topic of discussion was "Reporting on Celebrity." The editor of the *Los Angeles Times* caused quite a stir when he told me he would do something that just a few years ago was considered taboo for a respected newspaper: Put the story of Britney Spears's wedding on the cover of its entertainment section. Most of the stuffy academics in the audience almost spit-taked their English breakfast tea onto their fruit plates.

Celebrity has become the nation's single most powerful cultural force—in media, business and politics, where famous narcissists from Hilary Clinton to Arnold Schwarzenegger to Saddam Hussein are more interested in promoting their own celebrity than a significant political agenda.

"Barry's calling again," my bored assistant drones just a few minutes after his first call. "Line one."

I figured if it was an important call Bary would wait. I mean, now I was busy watching *Dr. Phil.*

BARRY POSNER

Special Assistant to the President

While I was sitting on the horn in silence, waiting for that pointy-nose paparazzo Tom Peppers to take my call, my colleagues over at the CIA were fighting the War on Terror. Meanwhile, I was miserable. I couldn't believe Dr. Rice ordered me to get this guy. It was just the latest proof that "military intelligence" had become an oxymoron.

When I first became an intelligence officer ten years ago, recruiting morons like Tom Peppers was not what I had in mind. But when you're a patriot, you often have to put aside your personal prejudices and do what's best for your country. I knew that Peppers possessed talents that none of us had in the CIA or over at the Pentagon. So I sucked it up. But did he really have to put me on hold for that long? It was a really bad start to what was fast becoming a really bad relationship. Problem is, I had no other choice. We were that desperate.

TOM PEPPERS

Hollywood Bureau Chief, *Them! Weekly*

In Hollywood, it's not so much rude to keep someone on hold as it is a sign of power and prestige. The longer you're able to keep someone dangling without them hanging up, the more power you have over them. It's the telecommunications equivalent of owning a Bentley convertible. It's status. I am an important guy in Hollywood. Washington has Tim Russert; Hollywood has Tom Peppers.

No other publication has contributed more to the celebritification of America than *Them! Weekly*. And I'm damn proud of it. Come to think of it, at the moment ole' Barry called, I was at the top of my game.

A lot of wonks and other assorted fuddy-duddies argue that our nation's obsession with the bold-faced names signifies some sort of cultural malady. These uptight intellectuals bemoan that the cult of the celebrity has become Americans' mainstream fetish, and that magazines like *Them!* serve mind candy to a populace that needs to consume much more protein-rich information. They make a good point, but people want to read this trash and I get paid a pretty penny to dish it to them on a glossy-paper platter. I am a public servant just as much as any government bureaucrat! Call me the chief advocate for celebrity-obsessed Americans, and my paparazzi are the eyes of America.

I oversee the entire news-gathering operation. Paparazzi stakeouts are at the top of my to-do list. I dispatch reporters to get information, through interviews and observations, that will give the photos context. I decide which pics are worth a hundred grand and which aren't worth a rat's ass. I have worked on hundreds of stakeouts, engineered thousands of pap shots, and I've ruffled many a celebrity feather along the way. That's what Gotcha Journalism is all about.

Luckily, my boss in New York always has my back. Her name is Bobby Lesser. I'm sure you've heard of her. The New York tabloids have portrayed Bobby as, at best, an evil genius and, at worst, "the devil," as Gwyneth Paltrow has called her. No matter what you think of her, she's a woman who in the span of just two years has transformed *Them!* from force. I've been Bobby's Hollywood guy throughout the *Them!* revolution, during which in less than three years we've quadrupled circulation. "Do whatever you have to do to win," she always tells me. And, almost always, I do.

Bobby and I get along famously. Maybe it's because she's three-thousand miles away and I don't have to bear firsthand her temper tantrums and wildly fluctuating mood swings. Or maybe it's that she trusts me to do my job, which I usually do better than anyone else in town. Or maybe it's because beneath my Boy Scout affability I'm as cut-throat, competitive and cunning as she is—though I'd never admit this.

In war, the element of surprise is key; if my enemies (the stars, the publicists, competing publications) knew I was so hard-core, I'd lose my edge. The fact that I'm just as dirty as the National Enquirer is my dirty little secret.

You might recall some of the best work I've done for *Them!*: Britney Spears making out with Colin Farrell at the Chateau Marmont, Cameron Diaz making out with Justin Timberlake on a surfboard, London Marriott (in—what else?—a micro mini-skirt) sitting spread-legged at the wheel of her Mercedes convertible revealing to the world what she was not wearing under her skirt. And did I tell you *Them! Weekly* was the first magazine to report that London Marriott had made a sex tape with her well-hung boyfriend? Yep, I broke that one too. Being jealous of my successes, my competitors at other magazines call me "Tabloid Tom."

I realize I'll never win the Pulitzer Prize for reporting, but at least I've got a hot wife and drive a Cadillac Escalade ... with tinted windows, of course.

LONDON MARRIOTT

Professional Celebrity

Tom Peppers is a total butt munch. I've heard they call him Tabloid Tom. But, I've seen it, girls, and it's more like Tiny Tom. And, like, you can quote me on that and stuff.

TOM PEPPERS

Hollywood Bureau Chief, *Them! Weekly*

I'm just the puppeteer pulling the strings of the paparazzi. I rarely take photos myself. But it is true that I've been known on occasion to sneak a digital with me to parties and snap an unsuspecting celeb. **Fabloid Editor Rule #2: Always carry a pocket-size digital.**

Mostly, though, I feed the photographers intelligence that allows them to, basically, just point and shoot. Finding celebrities is a cat-and-mouse game that requires all the craftiness of a CIA officer. I like to think of myself as Hollywood's top spy. Naturally, that's why those government Chachis came knocking.

I'm only thirty-two, but I feel like I've seen and done it all in this biz. In less than ten years I've gone from being a cub reporter to being Hollywood's top news editor. There ain't no shame to my game. I've sat outside Britney Spears's Santa Monica apartment for fourteen hours waiting for John Cusack to come out with his fly down (he eventually did). I've taken Kaballah classes pretending to be a convert to the Jewish cult just so I could get quotes from Ashton Kutcher and Madonna. I've attended AA meetings pretending to be an addict just so I could interview Courtney Love in rehab. I've stalked Demi Moore outside her Idaho ranch in order to nail a shot of her 40-year-old Botox-smooth cheek pressed against her sexy karate instructor's face. And I have even gone "dumpster diving." Sometimes the only way to find out what pills their popping is to find the empty bottles in their garbage. Hey, at least I wear gloves.

The key to any successful paparazzi mission is anonymity. If the star spots you, you get what we call "garbage"—that is, a boring shot. If they don't, you get gold. And just seven hours before our deadline, Julia Roberts—God bless her heart—had just given Them! gold. I knew Bobby was gonna love this one. Then the D.C. dorkmeister ruined all the fun. "Ken, it's Barry ... again," my bored assistant announced over the intercom for what seemed like the tenth time that morning. "Just take a message," I barked. "But he says it's really important," she shouted back into my office. Unless this dude was gonna tell me that Brad Pitt had just dumped Jennifer Aniston for their gay pool boy, I couldn't imagine this Barry dude would have anything to say I didn't already know. Plus, the reality was that I had like ten minutes to put in a bid on this Julia photo (starting at $10,000 and by the end of the day, after *People* had probably jacked up the price to $50,000, we'd have to out-bid or cut bait).

Ah, what the hell, I thought, I'll see what this guy has to say. To this day, I wonder what would have happened—to me, to our fucked-up country, to the people of Iraq, to my marriage, to the world—if I had not taken Barry's call.

BARRY POSNER

Special Assistant to President

There was an apocryphal story that started circulating around D.C. after Bush "won" the election. As the story goes, when Bush was promoted to lieutenant in the Texas National Guard back in the late 1960's, the ranking officer informed the draft-dodging son of a powerful senator of his new rank by saying, "Congratulations, lieutenant." To which Bush replied, "Thanks. But I'm not Lou Tenant."

I never believed the story. I always figured it was a bunch of Democratic drivel. But after Bush ordered me to recruit Tom Peppers, I started to believe it could be true. Bush just might be that dumb.

TOM PEPPERS

Hollywood Bureau Chief, *Them! Weekly*

"Y'ello," I finally answered, sounding annoyed and distracted, what we do in Hollywood to project the image that we have more important things to do than talk to you.

Barry had been on hold for thirteen minutes. As far as I was concerned, he could have used another thirteen to humble him adequately. But I had better things to do than power-play this bozo. Mr. Peppers," he said, rather politely. "Barry Posner here."

Who says "So-and-So here" anymore? Barry's voice sounded like a younger, more nerdy (if that's possible) Ben Stein's.

"Please pardon my persistence, but I work the federal government, and, uh, I'd really like to meet with you at your earliest convenience."

I assumed he was another propaganda-pushing bureaucrat trying to get the magazine to cover a fund-raiser being thrown by a bunch of Bush-backing celebs. Realistically, the only way I'd send a reporter to another one of these lame soirees was if Paris Hilton was on the guest list. You can be throwing a Tupperware party, but if Paris is on the guest list *Them!* will be there.

"No, I'm sorry. Paris Hilton is not involved," he replied.

"Okay then," I exhaled. "Just e-mail me the release." Just when I was about to give him the old take-care-and-buh-bye, Barry blurted out, "Please don't hang up! This isn't what you think. We have to talk."

"Who did you say you work for?" I asked.

Barry lowered his Ben Stein voice and said, "I work for the U.S. government, for the President."

"For the president of the United States?"

"Yes, Mr. Peppers, I do."

"George W. Bush?" I asked.

"Uh-huh. He's my boss."

"So you work in the White House?"

"No, the Old Executive Office Building," he said in the condescending tone of an adult on *Sesame Street.* "It's *next door* to the White House."

Condescending prick.

"I see," I replied, albeit skeptically. "You want me to believe that George Bush told you to call me?"

"Yes, Sir."

"You sure you've got the right Tom Peppers? I work for *Them!* magazine. I write about Hollywood crap, not politics."
"Trust me, we know who you are," he said. "That's why we have to meet."

I tried to figure out who were these "we" guys he kept talking about. Then I thought of something: Maybe Bush was pissed about the photo we'd run the week earlier of his daughter wasted in Mexico. (That was a doozy, I have to admit.) Or it could have been the IRS had finally caught on to all my bogus write-offs (last year alone: $1,678 for pens, $3,456 for a "business" trip to Miami Beach). Or maybe Attorney General John Ashcroft had decided that tabloid (or "fabloid," as I like to call purveyors of the glossier version of the tabs) journalists needed to be rounded up like al Qaeda and ensconced inside Columbia Journalism School to learn a more ethical brand of American Journalism.

Then I thought, Hey, I know what's going on! "Barry" was, in fact, Ashton Kutcher, and I was being played the fool on an episode of *Punk'd*!!!

"Hey, man" I said. "Be serious for a second. Is this Ashton Kutcher?"

"Ashton who?" he asked, sounding legitimately confused.

"So you are not Punking me?"

"Mr. Peppers," he said. "I couldn't be more serious."

BARRY POSNER

Special Assistant to the President

Paris Hilton! Tom Peppers gets a call from the Office of the President of the United States of *America* and all he wants to know is if Paris Hilton is involved! It's sad enough that I'd been ordered to recruit this pseudo-journalist for a job that we in the CIA could have handled ourselves. Now he was making a mockery of the entire thing.

Up until Operation Hollywood, I was on the perfect career track: Phi Beta Kappa in international relations at Georgetown. Three years at Stanford (where I studied under then-provost Condoleezza Rice, now the President's National Security Adviser, and my boss). Four years spying on Colombian drug lords for the CIA before I was caught in a flap, my cover was exposed, and the agency no longer deemed me "operationally viable."

I didn't join the CIA to take a desk job. I'm an *intelligence* officer, a spook, an expert in gathering valuable intelligence on our enemies. Recruiting tabloid journalists wasn't what I envisioned doing when I joined the CIA.

Don't get me wrong. I'd do just about anything for Ms. Rice. But when it entails calling upon a civilian—a tabloid journalist, no less—to help conduct a covert op (a blatant violation of Agency policy) I have to draw the line. I mean, I'm not a tour guide at Universal Studios. I did not become an intelligence officer to hire the unintelligent.

Not only have I undergone rigorous spy training (paramilitary techniques, surveillance, espionage detection), I even teach undercover tradecraft to CIA recruits at The Farm, the agency's secret training facility down in southern Virginia. I am an intelligence professional, and I take my job—to protect the security interests of our country and peace-loving people worldwide—very seriously. That's why recruiting Tabloid Tom was so hard on me. To be honest with you, on the integrity scale I rank celebrity journalists below funeral directors and FBI agents. They're scum.

CONDOLEEZZA RICE

National Security Adviser

I knew that until we captured Saddam Hussein the authority of the U.S military forces in Iraq would have been undermined, and our policy to rebuild a free and democratic Iraq forever comprised. For as long as the Iraqi resistance believed their leader might return to power the insurgents and die-hard Saddam loyalists would not cease their reign of terror—the suicide bombings, the sniper attacks, the daily terrorism to derail the nation-building process.

I couldn't have agreed more with what Secretary Powell said prior to the commencement of Operation Iraqi Freedom: "Saddam is a piece of trash that needs to be collected." Six months after the invasion to liberate the Iraqi people, the President had decided we needed to find better trash collectors. As the President said to me in private, "Colin is right. But you can't collect trash if you don't know where to find it." Consequently, it was evident that Tom Peppers was the nation's most qualified trash collector.

In a nutshell, that's why we launched Operation Hollywood. For the previous six months, we had employed every tactic, every high-tech tool at our disposal, all in an effort to take Saddam Hussein into custody and thus send a message to the Iraqi people that his evil regime would never again brutalize them.

We tried it all: Unmanned aircraft. Satellite imagery. Iraqi spies. Undercover agents. Door-to-door Special Forces raids. We offered a $25 million bounty to anyone who could give us information leading directly to Saddam's capture.

Yet Saddam Hussein remained at-large, a thorn in our collective sides free to release the periodic audiotaped address urging Iraqis to fight Coalition forces, which they were doing with vicious regularity. We'd made some progress. We'd set up the provisional authority, established military control of ninety percent of the nation, got the oil flowing again. A high point came a few months into the campaign when we killed Saddam's sons, Uday and Qusay. Yet, sadly, we had not gotten any closer to capturing their father.

There had been very few victories after that one. A major component of our challenge was that we live in a society of instant gratification. Our youth are addicted to video games in which a 10-year-old can literally destroy an entire city with the joystick of his virtual Apache. Ours is a culture of instant-messaging teenagers and cell phones and wireless e-mail devices. The backdrop to their lives is a media landscape of reality TV shows in which human conflict is created and resolved in the span of an hour-long episode.

We live in a society that, thanks to the vulgar volume of magazines and television programs communicating information about famous people, knows more about Oprah Winfrey's new house than the Speaker of the House.

The result of all these cultural maladies is a grossly shortsighted, ill-informed and impatient society focused on personalities rather than issues. Thus, the war in Iraq had become a fight between two celebrities—President Bush and Saddam Hussein— and until we captured Saddam I feared there would be no clear winner in the minds of the American people.

The press, as well as some of our political opponents, had started questioning the effectiveness of our special ops and of our entire military mission to bring peace and democracy to a nation that had never known either.

Most significantly, however, our allied coalition was growing impatient. Prime Minister Blair was running out of time, as the British people were losing faith in the war effort. I knew it wouldn't be long before the American public started asking the same questions and we found ourselves in yet another Vietnam: a war we don't have the will to win.

The President is an impatient man. He likes to see things get done, as he says, "right quick." As he had said at our last national security briefing, "I want Saddam captured by the New Year. Make it happen." That left us three months, and my job was to make it happen for him.

As the cliché goes, desperate times call for desperate measures. The President understood this; I understood this. And we believed that if the public ever found out what we undertook in order to achieve our goal they would understand.

I knew that if we achieved our goal—the capture of Saddam Hussein alive—it would go down as one of the most important military victories since World War II. We'd all be heroes of the highest order. Or at least that was the plan.

TOM PEPPERS

Hollywood Bureau Chief, *Them! Weekly*

The White House isn't exactly J. Lo's Miami mansion, but it's still pretty nice. Truth is, I had always wanted to work in the White House. Still, I never thought I'd ever step foot in it.

Back in the early '90s, when I was a bright-eyed journalism student at Columbia, I aspired to cover politics for a major metropolitan newspaper. Honestly, celebrity journalism was not my first-choice career. The real story is that I fell into this world after I failed to achieve my real goal: reporting for the *Washington Post.*

After getting out of school in 1994 I applied for dozens of entry-level reporter jobs. But while I had a master's degree from Columbia University, I had two major flaws: I was male and white. Okay, I had a serious third flaw: I was a crappy writer.

I watched as fellow graduates got great jobs and kick-ass internships, while I was forced to head back home, tail between my legs, and write obits and cover murders for my hometown paper, the *Smyrna News.*

But when I moved to Hollywood to be a freelance magazine writer I found liberation. To outsiders, L.A. is more superficial than a place like D.C. But it isn't. It just has different priorities—fame, looks, and money—than D.C., where college pedigree, family background, kissing the right asses and possessing arcane knowledge about public policy get you ahead.

Hollywood magazine editors simply want hustlers who get the story. That's why I thrived from the day I arrived. I still work harder than any journalists—even the tireless Bobby Lesser. My dad - God rest his soul—used to always say that idle hands are the devil's workshop. Dad worked in a print shop and never made more than $35,000 a year. Now I get paid six figures to do what I love: write and report news—albeit news about spoiled, rich actors. But I earn every cent.

Celebrity journalism is a blue-collar sport played by bare-knuckle types who aren't afraid to get their hands dirty. On the other hand, D.C. journalists, and the stuffy intelligentsia whom they cover, sit on their asses all day straightening their ties and adjusting their granny panties, churning out copy that makes

Parade Magazine look cutting-edge.

Looking back, I'm glad the *Post* shunned me that day ten years ago. I eventually found my calling out West, in L.A. to be exact, where I was able to reinvent myself as a celebrity journalist, a portrait of American transformational success. And when I wasn't feeling successful I could at least look up and see the sun shining.

And while newspapers struggle to keep readers, the business of glossy celebrity magazines is booming. At *Them! Weekly*, we had enjoyed a fifty-five percent newsstand sales every year for the last four years. Meanwhile, circulation at papers like the *Los Angeles Times* had remained flat. So while some people crucified Bobby Lesser as the devil, she was my savior.

THE OVAL OFFICE

3 October 2003

9:10 a.m.

RICE: Where's Mr. Peppers?

POSNER: Downstairs. He's in one of the cubbyholes down by the Situation Room. Here, take a look.

(Posner flicks on a security monitor.)

BUSH: Huh. Young guy. Sorta looks like Ellen Degeneres, don't he? He's got those Ryan Seacrest highlights.

POSNER: Yes, Mr. President, he is slightly androgynous.

BUSH: Androga what?

POSNER: Um, sir, what I'm trying to say is that his features aren't the most manly, that –

BUSH: You tryin' to tell me Mr. Peppers is a pretty boy?

POSNER: Yes, sir.

BUSH: Heck. Then why didn't you just say that in the first place?

POSNER: I apologize. Next time, I will.

RICE: Please, let's move on. Barry, did Mr. Peppers get approved for the highest security clearance?

POSNER: Yes, ma'am, I instructed the boys to make him Flash Project and got him fully cleared at TS/SCI.

RICE: What did you tell the CIA?

POSNER: That he was up for the press secretary job and we needed a backgrounder.

RICE: So Director Tenet has no idea why Mr. Peppers has been brought here?

POSNER: None at all.

RICE: Good work, Mr. Posner.

BUSH: Hey, guys, listen. I gotta go for a run. Laura says my butt is gettin' flabby, so I'm outta here for a bit. I'll be back in an hour. Bush out!

TOM PEPPERS

Hollywood Bureau Chief, *Them! Weekly*

Barry Posner did nothing but belittle me since I'd met him in the limo at Dulles.

"So, Tom, how long have you been in tabloid journalism," Posner snidely asked me on the way over to the White House. (Did I mention he has the annoying habit of talking through his teeth like Thurston Howell III?) "That's an *interesting* line of work for someone with an *Ivy League* degree."

"First of all, I don't work for a *tabloid*," I said. "I work for a *fabloid*."

"What's the difference?"

"*Them!* magazine is *fabulous*."

"And just what part of stalking people is so fabulous?"

I've debated the merits of celebrity journalism with eggheads like this before.

"Actually," I replied, "I consider my work patriotic."

Barry flashed a grin as wide as Dr. Phil and said, "That's one I haven't heard before."

"I'm exercising my First Amendment right," I continued. "I am a guardian of our right to free speech and a free press."

"I'm sure J. Lo sends her regards," he said, chortling like a pig.

I had to give the guy some credit, though. The best Hollywood journalists are able to get celebrities to tell them things they don't want to say. Some call it an interview, but I call it a manipulation. And Posner manipulated me. He convinced me to drop everything I was doing, let that Julia photo go to *People*, and walk down to the courtyard outside my office, where two burly Secret Service agents frisked me and drove me to the airport.

But now I was sitting in a conference room in the basement of the West Wing, a visitor's badge around my neck like those guys in *The West Wing*, realizing that if I was summoned here to explain my bogus tax write-offs I would be in an office over at the IRS, not at the White House. I realized that could only mean one thing: The President was pissed about those photos of Jenna.

THE OVAL OFFICE

3 October 2003

10:45 a.m.

(President Bush traipses into his office in a track suit, sweating from his morning jog.)

BUSH: Hey there, Condi. How ya doin'?

RICE: I'm fine, sir, thank you.

BUSH: Posey.

POSNER: Excellent, sir.

BUSH: Boy are my dogs barking! Hand me that glass, would ya?

(Posner hands the President a glass of orange juice, which the President promptly gulps down.)

BUSH: Ahhhh. Now we're talkin'! Okey-dokey, let's get started. Is he still here?

RICE: Yes, and Mr. Posner reported that we've got Mr. Peppers top-secret clearance. In fact, he's cleared for TS/SCI, Mr. President.

BUSH: What's that?

RICE: Top Secret Sensitive Compartmentalized Information. It's the same clearance all three of us in this room have—the highest.

BUSH: Hmm. SCI ... SCI. Sounds like that TV show now, don't it?

RICE: Sir, it's not, uh, . . . that's CSI.

BUSH: I knew that! Just kiddin' with ya, Condi. Lighten up, for Chrissakes. Laura's favorite show, I might add. ... Barry, why you rollin' your eyes?

POSNER: Contact lens. Sorry, sir.

RICE: Mr. President, Peppers has no idea why he's here. I think we'll be able to turn him.

BUSH: What makes you so sure?

RICE: For starters, this.
(Rice inserts a videotape into a VCR and on pops a grainy video of two people having sex in a hotel room.)

BUSH: Jumpin' jehusafat! That's not Jenna Jameson, is it?
RICE: No, sir. It's London Marriott, of the Marriott hotel fortune.
BUSH: Oh, yeah. Seen that gal on *Extra*. And who's the lucky fella?

POSNER: That's our man, Tom Peppers.

RICE: In the flesh, you might say.

POSNER: His wife doesn't know about this sex tape, sir.

RICE: What's your conclusion, Mr. President?

(Bush's eyes are glued to the screen.)

RICE: Uh, Mr. President.

BUSH (agitated): Hell, I hear ya, Condi. Jeesh. I'm thinking over here.

RICE: My point is that I think this tape will help Mr. Peppers understand how important it is that he joins our operation. We simply tell Mr. Peppers if he refuses to join our operation we will leak this video to one of the tabloids. I want him to know if he doesn't cooperate even worse things could happen.

BUSH: Like what?

RICE: We've done our homework on this guy, sir. We have a dossier an inch think on Mr. Peppers. He's got some serious skeletons. For starters, London Marriott isn't the only woman he's been with since he married.

POSNER: In fact, sir, our boys at CIA have confirmed a total of seventeen infidelities since me married his wife, Jessica, two years ago.

BUSH: What kind of girls is this guy poking?

POSNER (handing Bush the Peppers Dossier): Well, let me give you a sampling. It's your typical Hollywood scumbag profile. Sir, take a look:

```
Gina Thomas: American Idol intern. 21.
Blonde. Duration: 33 minutes.

Jennifer Kozner: Reality TV star. 24.
Blonde. Duration: 7.2 minutes.

Lindsey Bohan: Actress. 17. Auburn.
Duration: 14 minutes (of drunken action
in a limo).

Annabella Lindbergh: Norweigan TV
reporter. 29. Blonde. Duration: 66 days.

Drew Terrymore: Actress. 27. Blonde-ish.
Duration: 3 minutes.
```

POSNER: I think you're getting the picture, Mr. President.

BUSH: I most certainly am. This Peppers guy is a real Bill Clinton, ain't he? At least Peppers seems to have better taste in women!

POSNER: You might say that, sir.

BUSH: Okey-dokey then. But what about the boys at the CIA? You sure they don't suspect that we're up to somethin'?

RICE: They remain totally in the dark, sir. They have been effectively compartmentalized from this operation.

BUSH: What about Colin and Dick and Rummy and Karl Rove? These guys can't have even a whiff of what we've got up our sleeves.

RICE: Negative. Secretary Powell hasn't been briefed on this operation, nor has Karl Rove. Neither, of course, has the Vice President. In fact, sir, we've arranged for him to be at the cardiologist in Bethesda this morning.

BUSH: How is Dickie's ticker?

POSNER: I took the liberty of having the tech-geeks at HQ accelerate his pacemaker this morning, via remote control. So let's just say the Vice President's pulse was racing fast enough to scare him out to Bethesda.

BUSH: Well, don't go showin' him this tape! Dickie might have a freakin' coronary again on us! And definitely don't tell him about our little scheme.

RICE: Affirmative.

BUSH: Trust me, I know Dickie and those guys. They're little worry warts. And I'll tell ya this: If Dickie or Colin or Tenet or—God help us—that tight-ass Rummy find out about this operation - this *Operation Hollywood* - they'll want to hold a national security hearing or somethin' silly like that.

Rummy is so buy-the-book it kills me. He'd *squash* the plan, get the eggheads involved. Rover, he'd want to talk about the political risks till he was blue in the face. Heck, he'd want to take a poll or somethin'. As for Andy Card, just make sure he's focused on his job; he don't need to know jack-ola about this project. And, Colin, shoot, he'd never go for this. He can't accept that his old military boys just ain't gettin' the job done.

So what I'm saying is we can't let any of this out, you hear me? Condi, you and Barry can be the only two who know. Roger that?

RICE: Yes, sir.

BUSH: Laura doesn't even know, guys. So please don't mention anything to her. Please? I mean, if she found out what I was up to with these paparazzi, she'd slap my pee-pee somethin' fierce!

BARRY POSNER

Special Assistant to the President

I had been trying to stop this operation since Day One, when Ms. Rice first told me about the President's idea, and I told her it wasn't advisable—legally, politically or practically. Of course, as usual, no one listened to me.

Still, I felt passionately that someone had to stand up for those forgotten pillars of truth, justice, and the American way. I reminded Dr. Rice about what happened to Larry Deutch, the former CIA director, when he got himself into a mess of trouble back in '96.

Deutch told Congress that the Agency had been secretly recruiting journalists as agents. I wrote a paper on this subject at Stanford. Basically, in 1977 the CIA banned the practice, mostly because lefties convinced President Carter that the lives of American journalists abroad were at risk, and that foreign governments might execute legitimate journalist out of fear they were spooks. A lot of people in the media argued that recruiting journalists also could impair the ability of the press to function freely; in other words, Carter feared it might be unconstitutional, for it could be viewed as tinkering with the First Amendment rights of journalists. So they banned the practice. However, there was a loophole in the edict that allowed the president to waive the rule in "genuine and extraordinary circumstances," which is as vague as one can get. Essentially, it meant the president could okay the CIA to employ journalists whenever he felt like it. But when Deutch revealed that the Agency had recently used journalists he took a lot of heat.

I told Condi, "Politically, we would be attacked from all sides. Legally, the President could be impeached." I added, "And, practically speaking? Well, I don't think Tom Peppers will be any more skilled at hunting down Saddam than the CIA."

Dr. Rice was unmoved. She closed her briefing book and frowned at me, as if presenting a divergent view was suddenly anathema. "Before 9-11, I might have agreed with you, Mr. Posner. But we were caught asleep at the wheel. We were not prepared for the al Qaeda attacks. We played if safe, and we lost. Taking a conservative, safe approach to solving our military crises ended that day. If our enemies are willing to take the ultimate risk to kill us, we also have to take risks to meet the challenge."

I disagreed. But at the end of the day I respected her authority. And so, begrudgingly, that's why we called on Mr. Peppers.

TOM PEPPERS

Hollywood Bureau Chief, *Them! Weekly*

"You gotta be kidding me," I told the two uberwonks. "I wouldn't even know where to start looking for a guy like Saddam Hussein. And, pardon my French, but I can't ride a fuckin' camel."

"They drive cars in Iraq, Mr. Peppers," Rice replied, obviously not getting the joke.

In fact, Rice and Posner struck me as two of the most humorless people I'd ever met. Rice appeared thinner and taller than she looked to me on C-SPAN. But, thank God, she also was better looking. She has a gap between her two middle-front teeth that's wider than Letterman's, but even that's attractive. She's sexy in that pent-up, I-haven't-had-sex-in-ages-but-need-to kind of way. I have to admit that I probably would have done her, but Rice's constant lack of a visible smile threw any fantasy of us screwing on the oak desk all but impossible to visualize.

Posner's sitting posture, meanwhile, was so stiff I couldn't help but conclude he needed a good lay. Maybe that's the biggest difference why people in Hollywood are happier than D.C. nerds: We have more and better sex with more and better-looking people.

Posner opened a leather briefcase filled with what must have been a few dozen manila folders. "Don't worry, we can help you find him," he said, holding up a few of the folders. "We have all the cables here. Our analysts have narrowed the search down to a tiny circle of supporters who might be harboring him."

"All the legwork has been done," Rice added, suddenly cheerleader-peppy. "All you have to do is — "

"Is what?" I interrupted. "Do what the military and intelligence pros haven't been able to do? What makes you think I can do a job that everyone else hasn't been able to do?"

"Our military is great at dealing with enemies once we have located them," she said. "They aren't so good at what I'm told you are the best at: finding those who don't want to be found."

Rice's lips turned model pouty as she gazed down at her briefcase like a forlorn puppy. Just as my heart was melting, she strained her eyes upward and cracked a smile. "The president has specifically asked for you, Mr. Peppers," she said. "You're the man for the job."

She stared at me in silence. We'd blocked out Posner altogether. It was just me and Condi. I liked the way she locked her big, dark eyes onto mine. It was as primal as flirting can get with a Stanford Ph. D.

"But why me?" I asked her.

"The President said he saw you on that TV show about paparazzi," she said.

"The *Celebrity Hunt Club*?" I asked.

"Yes, that's it. I haven't seen it personally, but he was quite impressed with your work, couldn't rave enough about your keen ability to snuff out the enemy."

"Wow," I said, "I didn't know the president watched E!"

"He does, and he loves your work."

"Ms. Rice, can I ask you another question?"

"Yes."

"Can I call you Condi?"

"You can call me whatever you want."

DingleBarry's forehead veins were about to burst.

Condi definitely had done her research; I always fall for the flirting. But I believed she was nuts to think I could do the job, or at least I tried to make her think she was nuts. I like to think I drive a hard bargain.

"There's a big difference between finding Ben Affleck and finding Saddam Hussein," I reminded her.

"Not as much as you'd think," she replied. "We can give you more intelligence that will help you once you sign up for the job. Until then, we can't share any more details of our proposed operation other than to say it will involve photography. All we're asking is that you think of this as a patriotic duty. We need you, the President needs you, and, Mr. Peppers, your country needs you."

"Yeah, but my magazine also needs me," I said rather bluntly. I think she liked my attitude. "I can't lose my job over this." (I still owed $17,000 on my Escalade and about $1.5 million on my $1.8 million house in Manhattan Beach.) "And my boss isn't exactly the most understanding woman in the world."

"We will take care of the Bobby Lesser situation," Posner piped in from the end of the table. "Don't worry about her."

As Rice grabbed her leather briefcase and stood up I noticed how tight-fittingly sexy her knee-length skirt was on her. "Why don't you think about things for a few minutes, Mr. Peppers?"

As she strutted out the door (I'd never seen that skirt on C-SPAN), Posner, the lackey that he is, followed her—but not before dramatically dropping a manila folder in front of me like he was in a cheesy spy movie.

I opened it and inside was a VHS tape with a label reading, "London Marriott Tape."

"We'll leave you alone with this for a few minutes," Posner said, eyeing the VCR beside the flat-screen TV. "After you watch it, you might want to think *real hard* about whether you're going to join our operation."

THE OVAL OFFICE

3 October 2003

1:12 p.m.

(**Rice** and **Posner** enter to find the President at his desk giggling.)

RICE: What's so amusing to you, sir?

BUSH: Aw, heck, just a silly thought I had in my head.

RICE: Please share, Mr. President. We could use a little lightheartedness after that tense meeting with Mr. Peppers.

BUSH: Well, that's just it, this Peppers guy.

RICE: What about him?

BUSH: Hehehehe. I was just thinkin' how funny it would be if the guy had a Ph.D., or, say, if he was some sort of medical doctor.

RICE: Why's that, sir?

BUSH: Because then his name would be "Dr. Peppers." Ain't that a hoot!

POSNER: Oh, yes, that's a real laugh-riot, sir. Indeed, a *real* hoot.

BUSH: Okay, 'nuff funny business. How'd it go with, uh, *Mr.* Peppers?

RICE: He's resisting, as expected.

BUSH: Why for?

RICE: He doesn't think he can get the job done. He thinks we're setting him up to fail.

BUSH: You said he's cockier than a bull steer. What gives? Didn't you tell him *why* we need him. We need pictures, Condi! Tenet's boys ain't no photographers! That Predator drone aircraft certainly ain't gettin' the job done. We need real photographers. We need paparazzi, I'm tellin' ya. Have you told Peppers all this?

RICE: No, sir, not yet. We haven't mentioned the specifics of the photography.

BUSH: Why the hell not?

RICE: Don't worry, Mr. President.

BUSH: But I *am* worried! Don't forget, Condi, I won the election by the skin of Jeb's hanging chad. We need to get Saddam before the Democrats can make it an issue in the election.

RICE: I understand. But we can't reveal the depth of—or lack of—intelligence on Saddam's whereabouts until he agrees to join the operation. We can't risk the security breach, sir.

POSNER: I don't think we have anything to worry about. Something makes me think he'll come around.

BUSH: Oh, yeah? Why's that, smarty pants?

POSNER: Well, as I walked out of the room I handed him the tape.

BUSH: The sex tape?

(Posner nods "yes")

BUSH: 'Atta boy, Posey. I knew there was a reason we put ya in charge. Come over here and give your president a high five!

TOM PEPPERS

Hollywood Bureau Chief, *Them! Weekly*

In Hollywood, fear gets things done. It's the town's single greatest motivating force. Fear that a competing studio will steal your movie idea. Fear that if you don't get your picture taken on a red carpet the public will soon forget about you. Fear that if you don't give a magazine an interview they'll print nasty things about you.

As much as I hate to admit it, those D.C. pansies were scaring me into joining. But I wasn't about to let them beat me at my own game . . . without a fight.

BARRY POSNER

Special Assistant to the President

I've never been a big fan of blackmail. I think it's a cheap way to coerce someone into doing something against their will. The first rule of espionage is to identify and recruit people who need very little persuasion. Then you just find what they want and make it happen for them. If it's money, you give them it. If it is an American passport, you give them that. In Panama once I needed to hire a local pilot to infiltrate one of the drug-running cartels. We'd already gathered evidence that the pilot was running drugs for a different cartel, and I easily could have threatened to jail him if he didn't work with us. But, like I said, these kind of recruiting tactics are cheap, the work of lazy intelligence officers who don't have the people skills to persuade people to turn.

Anyway, turns out that the pilot, Eduardo, who only knew how to fly single-engine Cessnas, had always dreamed of taking flight lessons for a 747. So, of course, I made a deal that he would get those flight lessons if he worked undercover for us. When it comes to recruiting, your best bet is always to create a win-win situation. That's why I was against leaking the Tom-and-London sex tape.

But I couldn't do anything about it. I had to pick my battles. This Operation Hollywood was going to test my patience for bureaucratic incompetence, and I couldn't fight Dr. Rice on every point—especially when the president endorsed it.

When I returned to the SIT room, I tried my best to persuade Tom. But he was too feisty for his own good.

"You fuckers think you can blackmail me, don't you?" he shouted across the table as he paced. "You think you can scare me into joining. Well, you don't know who you are dealing with."

"Listen, Tom," I tried to reason with him. "All we're saying is that we know about the tape. Last I checked, knowing something is not blackmail. It just means we know something."

"What? That I banged London Marriott? Do you really think that I am going to be ashamed about banging the most-banged girl in Hollywood? I'm a celebrity journalist, not a Baptist minister! There is no shame to my game."

"Okay," I replied, trying to save him from himself. But it was no use. “So what should I tell Dr. Rice?”

He stood up and handed me the tape. “Tell her to take a look at this video. It just might loosen her up a little.” As Peppers reached for the door to leave, he added, “And tell her to fuck off.”

Like I said, I tried to save him. I really did.

October 10, 2003

NEVERWOOD CLINIC

Where we take the wood out of Hollywood

To: Bobby Lesser, Editor in Chief, *Them! Weekly*

From: Marty M. Friberg, Director, The Neverwood Clinic

Re: Tom Peppers's treatment program

The purpose of this letter is to inform you that your employee, Tom Peppers, has begun a three-month treatment for sex addiction at the world-famous Neverwood Clinic in Hermosa Beach, California, and thus will be unable to return to work until January 10, 2004.

Just like hundreds of Hollywood celebrities before him (including Charlie Sheen, Arnold Schwarzenegger, Simon Cowell, and, believe it or not, Ray Romano of Everybody Loves Raymond), we expect Mr. Peppers to make a total and complete recovery while a patient in our patented WoodShed™ program.

To verify the extent of Mr. Peppers's hypersexual peccadilloes, enclosed is an exclusive copy of the videotape of Mr. Peppers engaging in numerous sex acts (some of which are illegal in several Southern states) with professional celebrity London Marriott. Thanks for your understanding in this matter. We at Neverwood wish your magazine continued success during Mr. Peppers's temporary medical leave.

BOBBY LESSER

Editor in Chief, *Them! Weekly*

I should know better than anyone that looks can be deceiving. I mean, if someone based their opinion of me solely on what they read in the *New York Post*, they'd think I was the second coming of Tina Brown, which I am not. She's a dreadful woman, full of herself, just out to make a buck no matter whose lives she tramples on. But at *Them!* we care about the stars. We're not a tabloid that goes and writes whatever it wants about a celeb. We have a team of reporters and fact-checkers whose sole job is to make sure that readers learn the truth about the personal lives of these public people. We created a genre—the fabloid—that now everyone is copying. We've revolutionized journalism. And Tom Peppers, my point man in Hollywood, has played a major role in the *Them!* revolution.

But I have to admit that I would never have thought in a million years that Tom Peppers of all people was a sex addict (not to mention, Ray Romano; that's just a shocker!). If anything, Tom had always seemed like the consummate professional and, actually, often *uninterested* in women.

I remember looking at hundreds of photos from last fall's Victoria's Secret runway show with him and not once did Tom even give a hint that the models were drop-dead gorgeous. He might as well have been looking at a floor tile catalogue. Most straight guys wouldn't have been able to get through the photo-select without at least one off-color sexual comment. But not Tom. He was always a pro, focused on the job to an almost scary degree. But I hear sex addicts are like serial killers. It's always the quite ones.

I do suppose, however, that the sex tape from the anonymous tipster said it all. That London Marriott is quite the sex pistol! (And I didn't realize Tom had such a cute butt!)

I was not worried about our magazine, though. I had faith that we'd endure the crisis of not having Tom around for the a few months while he underwent treatment for his sex addiction. Tom had built a great team of journalists out in L.A. who could keep chasing down the stars and keep the gossip flowing in. There was a template in place.

I just wished Tom a very speedy recovery, and, of course, I felt sorry for his wife. Jessica was a saint, that woman, sticking with him even through his time of crisis.

You have to look on the bright side, that's my motto. At least I had some juicy cover lines to play with for our next few issues. Any story involving sex and London Marriott is always a bona-fide bestseller.

But I sincerely did wish Tom the best of luck and health throughout his recovery. I would have prayed for him, if I were at all religious.

TOM PEPPERS

Hollywood Bureau Chief, *Them! Weekly*

You've got to hand it to the wonks. They went and took a page right out of the Hollywood publicist handbook, crafting a totally-untrue-but-believable story. I was no more a sex addict for having sex with London Marriott than George Bush was a world leader just because he held the title of President. All that videotape proved was that I'm a male—a horny, flawed, red-blooded American dude. And, last time I checked, that wasn't a crime.

My good friend Joe Francis—the boy-genius behind those *Girls Gone Wild* videos—knows better than anyone how things work in Hollywood. Joe once told me, "You haven't made it in Hollywood until you've banged Tara Reid and London Marriott."

Please don't misunderstand me. I'm well aware that it's wrong to cheat on your girlfriend or, in my case, my wife. But, c'mon, let's be real here. A high-profile Hollywood guy like me having sex with London Marriott is like being handed a hot towel at a sushi bar. You get one just for showing up.

LONDON MARRIOTT

Professional Celebrity

When Barry Posner first approached me—like, a month or whatever before I did the deed—I almost threw up. Not that throwing up is a bad thing; I mean, how do you think I keep my bikini body?

It's just that Tom has almost no muscle tone, and he's such a ... well, such a total dorkster. All my friends who had ever seen him on E! thought he looked like a male Ellen Degeneres, which is not exactly, well, hot. Plus, what is he? Like thirty-five or whatever? Total oldster.

It's a woman's purgatory to change her mind, though. So when Barry Posner told me what I'd get in return for the tape. I couldn't say no. A girl can only do so much Ecstasy, party her ass off at so many clubs, be the star of so many hot reality shows, sleep with so many hot guys, and, believe it or not, wear so many cute outfits. Okay, so maybe you can't wear enough cute outfits. But, still, after a while every girl needs a new challenge, something new that gets her juices flowing, so to speak. And, you know, everyone needs to do things for a higher purpose and stuff like that. So when I look back, having sex with Tom Peppers was, like, my cervical duty.

TOM PEPPERS

Hollywood Bureau Chief, *Them! Weekly*

I'm well aware that most anyone would think I was a dirty, rotten pig of a man, that I was just as reckless and self-centered for "checking into" the London Marriott as any of the misbehaving men who'd done the same before me. Most everyone will probably assume I was a bad husband, a shady journalist and, judging by my highly sloppy sex with London, a bad lover (in my defense, I *was* wasted out of my mind!).

I don't blame anyone for thinking I'm a cad. In fact, I might not have been a big enough man to stop myself from exploiting celebs all those years, but at least I am big enough to admit to you today that I'm guilty on all counts. For years, I'd been masquerading as a self-proclaimed Celebrity Truth Detector, a tattletale going around town documenting all the illicit things the supposedly squeaky-clean stars did when not wearing their million-dollar smiles and $100,000 gowns on the red carpet. Suddenly, everyone in the world knew I was a hypocrite, focusing on other people's missteps in order to conceal my own shortcomings.

That night with London humbled me. While it might have been the best four-and-a-half minutes of my sexual career, that didn't really matter. I had been busted, exposed for all the world to see. And while ninety-nine percent of the heterosexual American male population envied me, I was not very proud of myself.

It shook me awake from my decadent slumber amid the celebrity slimeballs. And the truth is that, for all his annoying, condescending and corrupt ways, I had to thank that stumpy man Barry Posner for inspiring my conversion. I became a born again Good Guy. Amen, hallelujah! Praise London! Seriously, if every man slept with London Marriott I honestly believe the world would be a better place.

LONDON MARRIOTT

Professional Celebrity

Getting Tom to sleep with me wasn't, like, a challenge or anything. Like, didn't Tom ever hear of playing hard to get? Seriously! Myself, I like challenges, and that's exactly why I couldn't wait to start my new job in Washington.

What also was really cool to me was that I'd never been to Washington, actually. I'd always dreamed of living in Washington—all those Christmas trees, guys in flannel shirts, the clean air and green mountains. But I heard it rained a lot up there, which was not cool at all. I like to lay out. I do not fake bake - ever.

But my sister totally cheered me up when she told me that Washington had really awesome shopping, had lots of trees and mountains and was close to Vancouver. It's so weird, though. I don't think I saw any mountains or a nice shop my entire time in Washington. So, on that score, it kind of sucked.

TOM PEPPERS

Hollywood Bureau Chief, *Them! Weekly*

Just put yourself in my shoes for a minute: London Marriott comes up to me at the after-party for Ryan Seacrest's New Year's Eve show on FOX. We're in a dark club at the Hard Rock. I was feeling no pain at all when she asked me for a light, which, of course, I didn't have since in Hollywood smoking is only done by actresses who want to stay skinny. Staring at London's little B-cups advertising themselves as subtly as a whore on Hollywood Boulevard, I was motivated to get some matches from the bartender. That's when she moved in for the kill. As I lit her cigarette, she grabbed my hand and, over the roar of the party, whispered ever-so-softly in my ear, "Hey, Tommy, you wanna bang the box?"

Seriously. I am not kidding. She really asked me that! Now, A) I had never heard that phrase before. And B) I had never had a woman so hot offer me sex so quickly! It's not like I'm the ugliest guy in the world, but, let's face it, I'm not so good looking that hot chicks just walk up and ask me if I want to, uh, "bang" their "box."

In retrospect, I should have known something was up the second I stepped inside her hotel room. The giveaway should have been that, right as I was about to commit adultery, London says in that whiny voice of hers, "The lighting fucking sucks in here." I thought that was suspicious. But, being wasted and horny, I ignored it. Needless to say, the rest was fucking history. Literally.

LONDON MARRIOTT

Professional Celebrity

I knew I'd get revenge on Tom Peppers. From that day he went on Howard Stern and told everyone about my first sex tape, the one with that creep ex of mine, it made me want to die. It was sooo embarrassing. After Tom did that exposé in *Them!*, everyone else in the media covered it. I knew right there that I'd get that little prick.

To this day, everyone asks me how he was in bed. And I'll be totally honest with you: I've had better, but I've definitely had worse. But at the end of the day I would totally do it again. It was like I slept my way to the top. How cool is that?

TOM PEPPERS

Hollywood Bureau Chief, *Them! Weekly*

That *Them!* cover with me and London sold over a million copies that week. Which meant I got the usual thousand-dollar bonus for hitting the holy grail: the million-copies mark on the newsstand sales. Only I wasn't celebrating. I had fucked up. Besides having a weakness for slutty blondes, my fatal flaw was that I forgot celebrity journalism's guiding principle: The truth always comes out.

It's a good thing I had to leave for Iraq in just two weeks, because the day that cover came out I officially became homeless. Jessica kicked me out of the house, even though, mind you, it was *my* house. But Jessica had me by the balls.

I hate hotels, so I crashed at Jaimee P.'s apartment in Santa Monica while I worked on getting ready for the mission in Iraq. At least I had one friend who hadn't totally disowned me. Jaimee is a good girl, not to mention the best female paparazzo in town.

I wanted to make some good out of all the bad. The mission in Iraq was my chance to earn back some of the positive karma I'd lost over the years while sucking celebrity blood. I wanted to use my skills for good, rather than evil. I decided that if adultery and sleeping with the enemy was my sin, then finding Saddam Hussein would be my penance.

JAIMEE P.

Celebrity Photographer

I don't care who the guy's had sex with, because I know that Tom Peppers is a good man. London Marriott is a ho bag, anyway. She probably dropped Viagra in his drink or something. She's such a spoiled bitch. I can't even go into it, she pisses me off so much.

The bottom line is that Tom was the first guy in this town who cared more about looking at my photos than looking at my ass. That's rare in this town, and I'll always be grateful to him for that.

I mean, nobody's perfect—especially guys. Let's face it, they're all dogs. I think Uma Thurman said it best after she caught Ethan Hawke cheating on her when she told Howard Stern, "All men are pigs." I'd have to agree with that. Why do you think, at 27, I'm still single? There's no one worth my time.

All I know is that Tom cares about the truth, and that's what he sees in my photos: honesty. The first shot I ever sold him was one I took of that dreadful Gwyneth Paltrow parking her Range Rover in a handicapped spot in front the Starbucks at 7th and Montana. I was new to the business, little more than a stalker with a point-and-click camera and a knack for spotting celebrities on the street. But Tom didn't care about my lack of credentials; he only cared about the photo.

I'll never forget what happened when he first saw it. I was afraid he'd tell me it wasn't any good, that it wasn't framed properly, that the light was poor. But he looked at the print and instantly told me, "This tells me more about Gwyneth Paltrow than a million magazine interviews ever have." Tom is a brilliant man. He sees the big picture in a town obsessed with the small picture. I love him.

My father wanted me to go to law school. But I'd come to realize that we lived in an age of images. I believe that the people who control the images also control the information; thus the image-makers have all the power. And, to be honest with you, that's why I think a lot of celebrities resent the paparazzi. It's not because we're invading their private space. They want to see their pictures in magazines. The problem is that paparazzi photos reveal their true selves, and, well, I guess some of them can't always handle the truth.

I always believed in Tom. Was he perfect? No. Who is these days? Show me a perfect person and I will show you a scam artist. If I've learned anything in Hollywood, it's that the only "normal" people are the ones you don't know very well.

TOM PEPPERS

Hollywood Bureau Chief, *Them! Weekly*

Jaimee P. is one of the best paparazzi out there. Being the only female, she's also the cutest. But, most important, she's a good person, a rarity in this business. Jaimee really thinks she's saving the world by taking pictures of celebrities. The truth was that if that's her goal she should have been taking pictures for *National Geographic*. But I was not going to tell her that. She was too good to lose.

The only reason she's shooting celebs is because she's hung up on her famous sister. Yeah, her sister's an actress, a real, big, famous one who has won an Academy Award. She is blond, gorgeous and really rich. Everyone loves her—except for Jaimee. Jaimee, who is shorter, a little chunkier, and has shorter hair, hates her sister's guts because she thinks she's a phony baloney. Jaimee would kill me if she knew I told you, but, for the sake of full disclosure, I will let you in on a secret: Her sister is Gwyneth Paltrow. That's right. The "P" stands for Paltrow.

JAIMEE P.

Celebrity Photographer

I grew up in Brentwood , surrounded by stupid celebrities, so I know how fake they are. I know how they manipulate the public into thinking that they are, say, cool, alternative types when they're really just spoiled rich brats. I know how much bullshit all that Hollywood crap is.

Between the publicist spin, the slick studio marketing campaigns, the airbrushed magazine covers, the scripted "reality" TV shows, and the studio photo-shoots, it's getting harder to distinguish reality from fantasy. I don't want to get into it too much, but let's just say I've seen firsthand this bogus star-making machinery in action.

There's one star, whom I will not name, who's considered one of the top film actresses. I saw her go from being a gawky, hook-nosed teenager whose only talent was having a father who was friends with Steven Spielberg, to being a nose-job-repaired celebrity with a ten-million-dollar asking price. I saw the plastic surgery, the team of image consultants who concocted her "life story" and made sure a dishonest *People* magazine profile made it public record. They built her up as this sweet, smart, sophisticated, vegan young woman when in fact she spent most of her time eating hamburgers and blaming her plastic surgeon for not giving her Angelina Jolie's bee-stung lips. This vile person, who shall remain nameless, now is considered America's Sweetheart. It makes me want to barf. If the American public only knew the real story . . .

The paparazzi are society's only true reality-checkers. If anything, Tom had done more for the cause of Truth than any other journalist since Woodward and Bernstein. I'd go as far to say that if more journalists covered Washington politicians like Tom Peppers and the *Them!* crew does Hollywood stars we might not have that fool George Bush in office because the public would have known how ill-prepared he really was for the job. There would have been photos of him spanking asses and swilling beer in Houston bars. There would have been photos of his loser daughters smoking crack in the back-alleys of Austin.

I really didn't care what they were saying about Tom. I'd do anything for the guy. I'd let him stay at my apartment as long as he needed. Sure, that sex-tape scandal hurt him. But one thing about Tom that I've always admired was his eternal optimism. If someone said it was impossible to get a shot of Angelina on the set of her new movie, he'd find a way to get one. He's living proof that all moves are possible on the human chessboard.

INSIDE THE ACTORS STUDIO ... WITH JAMES LIPTON

The New School Theatre, Manhattan, NY

08 June 2003

LIPTON: Tonight, we have a very special treat for all of you, my ignorant theatre students. Our actor in the chair tonight with us has brought to full, Technicolor life a host of characters as diverse as the colors of the rainbow. This gracious woman has inspired us all with her courage, her talent, as well as her impassioned views on the state of American politics. She has played a young woman who impersonates a boy in order to act in Shakespeare's plays; she has played a suicidal rich girl in bad need of Prozac; and, most recently, she has played the role of yoga-practicing groupie for the British band Coldplay. Ladies and gentleman, without further ado, please join me in welcoming the one and only, the uplifting and eponymous, the beautiful and brilliant, the incomparable Ms. Gwyneth Paltrow.

(Wild applause)

PALTROW: My gosh, you are all too kind. Please, please. Thank you from the bottom of my heart. I am going to blush. Golly. Gee. Thank you! I love you all!

(More wild applause)

PALTROW: Thank you all so very much. I am not worthy. Thank you all.

LIPTON: No, thank *you*, Gwyneth —

PALTROW: Call me Gwen.

LIPTON: Okay, thank you, Gwen, for gracing us with your elegant presence.

PALTROW: It's my pleasure.

LIPTON: No, it is ours. Before opening the floor to questions from our assembled acting students, I absolutely would be remiss if I didn't ask you a few questions about your craft. So, if I may –

PALTROW: You most certainly may.

LIPTON: Well, Gwen, I have been absolutely dying to ask you, How does if feel to be literally on top of the world?

PALTROW: Well, I know this may sound cliché and somewhat trite, but, Mr. Lipton, it is lonely at the top. I would never, ever ask anyone to feel sympathy for a famous, rich, gorgeous, successful actress, but I would not be telling you the whole truth if I didn't express the pitfalls that come with all that fame and fortune.

LIPTON: My dear, please do share, your words are the wisdom that we all aspire to live by.

PALTROW: Well, like most actors, I entered the profession so that I could inhabit these wonderfully complex worlds created by Hollywood's brightest writers, but in doing so I myself have become the story, rather than the characters being the story. The media, alas, has stricken me with the disease of Celebrity.

LIPTON: Why do you suppose this happens so frequently, Gwen? Is it a veritable cultural sickness, in which the masses worship these celebrities and focus on their lives in order to live in denial about their own pathetic existences?

PALTROW: Perhaps, Professor Lipton. But most of all I have to lay most of the blame squarely on the media. Especially the paparazzi. From the moment the Academy bestowed on me the Oscar for best actress for my work in *Shakespeare in Love* –

(Wild, gushing applause!)

PALTROW: Thank you all so very much. As I was elucidating, from that magical Oscars moment in 1997, I have not been able to enjoy a private moment without the prying lens of the paparazzi viewing it. It's just awful. They don't realize that their constant voyeurism can ruin lives. I mean, I've had my relationships with Brad Pitt and Ben Affleck ruined by the poisonous speculation and invasive paparazzi photographs that are propagated by tabloid magazines. It's just dreadful.

LIPTON: I am told you are embarking on something of a political crusade over this issue.

PALTROW: Indeed. This focus on personality above anything else has infected the world of politics, and that is why I believe it is time we take a stand. We live in a world where the CNN's, the FOX News's, the MSNBC's of the world make us more obsessed with the personalities of politicians rather than their policies, which are actually what impact our lives most.

LIPTON: Gwen, please let me ask you: Who in the media is most responsible for this celebritification of America?

PALTROW: No one person in the media is more responsible for this sick trend than the editor of *Them! Weekly*, Bobby Lesser. She is, in fact, the devil.

I would go as far as to contend that this is the main reason why our nation has in the White House a horrible man such as George W. Bush, a man who has no compassion for the plight of the poor and downtrodden and the defenseless trees and animals as I do. Yet President Bush was elected simply because he seemed like a cooler, more likeable guy than Al Gore. Rather than having a system about the politics of policy, it has become about the politics of celebrity. This disease that began in Hollywood has now infected the halls of Washington, and it is very disturbing to all of us. As a celebrity, I feel compelled to stand on the soap box that has been placed before me and shout, "Enough already!"

LIPTON: You are an absolutely awesome human being. Please continue to let your melodious locution grace our ignorant ears. Please, continue.

PALTROW: My friends, I sit before you tonight believing with all my heart that acting remains the single most important thing a human being can do in service to the world. But being a celebrity is different than being an actor. The two are mutually exclusive. Acting is God's greatest gift. But being a celebrity is like having a disease for which there is no cure.

LIPTON: I believe I speak for all of your fans around the world when I say to Bobby Lesser and nasty tabloid journalists like her, "Shame on you! Shame on you for distracting her—and us—from her craft! Shame on you, tabloid people!"

(The crowd starts chanting, "SHAME ON YOU! SHAME ON YOU!")

LIPTON: Please, please, please, students! Your passion is appreciated, but we must stop this heathen chanting. After all, we are actors, refined human beings, who find more acculturated ways to express our emotions.

Back to you, Gwen. As perhaps the most intelligent leading lady ever to be imprinted on celluloid, what would you propose be done to eradicate this cult of celebrity, as it were?

PALTROW: I actually have given this a lot of thought, Professor Lipton. And, if I may, I would like to use my appearance tonight on your show to announce a new initiative that I, along with my colleagues Julia Roberts, Jennifer Aniston, Carmen Electra,

Pamela Anderson and Arnold Schwarzenegger, will be taking to Washington, D.C., in the coming months. We are proposing a bill, sponsored by the entire congressional delegation from the state of California, that will make it a crime to photograph a famous actor anywhere outside of a movie/TV/or music video set. Our bill would make it a felony. We are calling our crusade, "Save Our Actors."

(More applause from the inspired acting students!)

LIPTON: Good for you, Gwen. How else can the American public support the passage of this bill into law?

PALTROW: There are two things they can do. One, they can stop buying the magazines and trashy TV shows that publish these destructive images claiming to show "the real" person behind the images we work so hard to manufacture. And, two, they can go to www.SaveOurActors.org, where they can send a letter of support to their local congressional representative.

LIPTON: Well, I must say that you, Ms. Paltrow, have inspired, educated and awakened all of us here tonight. You are a goddess among us mortals. Before closing, would you like to add anything else?

PALTROW: Yes. Go see my new film *Tongues Afire*! I play Vin Diesel's lesbian girlfriend who unwittingly gets caught in an international porn ring that leads to my kidnapping, only to be saved by Vin in the end. It opens wide on four thousand screens next weekend. It's a kick-ass movie.

LIPTON: Ms. Paltrow, we salute you!

**** TOP SECRET ****

For the President only

20 October 2003

To: George Bush, The President of the United States

From: Karl Rove, White House Chief Political Strategist

Re: The news weeklies report

Weekly Magazine Newsstand Sales Report

Mag.	**Cover Line**	**Copies Sold**
Them!	"London's Lies!"	[3,456,777]
Us	"Jessica's Secrets"	[1,495,002]
People	"J Lo or J Ho?"	[1,100,345]
InTouch	"Britney's Boys"	[487,233]
Newsweek	"Viagra Miracles"	[469,869]
Time	"Bush v. Saddam"	[327,345]

WHITE HOUSE SOUTH LAWN JOGGING TRACK

22 October 2003

10 a.m.

BUSH: Hey, Rover. Where've you been, buddy?

ROVE: Breakfast, sir.

BUSH: Beautiful day, ain't it? Nothin' but blue skies smilin' at me. You know, that's a line in a Lyle Lovett song.

ROVE: Oh.

BUSH: Yep. Did ya know that Lyle's from Texas?

ROVE: No, I didn't, sir.

BUSH: Rover, ya really gotta get with the program.

ROVE: I will, sir. I've already begun reading *Them! Weekly*.

BUSH: Well, that's a good start. Hey, tell me somethin', Karl. So why aren't you joggin' with me?

ROVE: Sir, I haven't run since college. And, well, let's face it: I'm thirty pounds overweight and have a bum knee.

BUSH: Heck, maybe if you got off that golf cart you'd drop some pounds. I told the same thing to Powell; he's lookin' a little soft in the middle too. Damn workaholic, that guy. Too work-focused. Not havin' enough fun, if you know what I mean. You gotta enjoy life, Rover.

ROVE: I'll take it into consideration, sir.

BUSH: Good. Hey, man, I read that memo I asked for, the one about the weekly magazine sales. It got me thinkin'. Thinkin' about the *mood* of the American people.

ROVE: Of course. That's why we also conduct polls, to gauge the mood of the voters, to help you make better decisions on behalf of the American people.

BUSH: Well, screw the polls! In fact, just stop doin' them altogether.

ROVE: But, but –

BUSH: But nothin'. Where have the polls gotten me? My

approval rating is sinking faster than my daddy's after the first Gulf war. From now on, Karl, the only numbers I want to see are the weekly magazine sales figure. Got me?

ROVE: Yes, I understand, but I must contend that the magazines are a flawed sample of –

BUSH: I don't want to hear it, Karl. Look here. How much are people plunkin' down for those magazines? It's like three bucks, ain't it?

ROVE: I believe it's even more than that, on the order of $3.29.

BUSH: Well, then, if people do vote with their pocketbooks, I want to know what's getting' them to open their pocketbooks. It's only common sense. Not enough *common sense* in this town, Karl. That Beltway is cutting off the blood flow to your heads.

ROVE: But, Mr. President, those are just magazines, celebrity rags that have nothing to do with –

BUSH: Shut yer' pie hole, Rover. I don't care. Made up my mind. Not changin' it. Can't talk me out of this one, like you did when I wanted to change the name of liberated Iraq to BushLand. But I ain't budgin' on this. Get it done.

ROVE: Okay, sir.

BUSH: Oh, and another thing, Karl: Kick those reporters from *Time* and *Newsweek* out of the front row in the briefing room. From now on, I only want *Them!* seated in the front row. That magazine is what people are readin' anyway, it's what real Americans care about. And, now that I'm thinkin' of it, while you're at it tell our PR flacks that when we capture Saddam—and, mark my words, we will capture this Butcher of Baghdad—I expect to be on the cover of *Them!*. Hear me on that?

ROVE: Whatever you say, Mr. President.

BUSH (stopping to drink water): And make sure London starts tomorrow. We really could use her 'round here. This staff could use a little kick in the pants.

ROVE: Whatever you say, sir. But are you sure of this?

BUSH: Sure as shit.

ROVE: Okay then.

BUSH: Good. Now get your fat ass off that golf cart and join me for a jog.

ROVE: Can't sir.

BUSH: Why not?

ROVE: Um, sir. I have to crap.

TOM PEPPERS

Hollywood Bureau Chief, *Them! Weekly*

"I quit," I told DingleBarry in a tone as flat as Dick Cheney's personality.

Barry goes, "But you ... you ... you ... "—the poor, flustered bastard!—"you can't quit. You aren't even signed on yet."

DingleBarry kept pushing his glasses up his fat, oily nose, but they'd slide back down every time.

"Oh, yeah," I returned volley like an eight-year-old. "Watch me."

I walked out of the drab government building and into the dry desert air. It's bad enough I wasted a day of my life driving all the way to this ugly-ass military base near Barstow. One other thing that was for sure was that I was not going to Iraq for three months. I told Barry, "I'm going to risk my life to help you hapless government fucks find some goober you should have found on your own."

Running like Richard Simmons, Barry finally caught up with me in the parking lot as I'm about to get into my car. The twenty-yard sprint had caused like three dozen beads of sweat to start racing down his pudgy face.

"But if you don't sign the commitment papers," he threatened me, "they will release other dirt on you."

I pretended I didn't care that they would reveal that I had slept with seventeen women (who weren't my wife) in a span of two years. I pretended that it wouldn't ruin my marriage and my career and, not to mention, embarrass the shit out of my mom.

"I'll take my chances," I said before climbing into my Escalade and spitting sand in his face.

BARRY POSNER

Special Assistant to the National Security Adviser

I'd never tell this to her face, but I blamed Dr. Rice for the mess we were in with Peppers. She should have told Tom Peppers just how awful our intelligence was from the get-go. Things at the CIA were so bad that they'd stooped to gathering intelligence by watching CNN. Seriously, for a time there, it was as if Wolf Blitzer was the CIA's Baghdad bureau chief.

In that first White House meeting with him, Dr. Rice shouldn't have made it seem like we at least had *some* idea where Saddam is hiding. The best intelligence we had was from a former guard in Saddam's Special Security Service whom we had recently interrogated. They called him the Fat Man. This so-called Fat Man claimed Saddam was being ferried around the country in taxis, wearing various disguises, and sometimes even driving the taxicab himself. That was the best intelligence we had to date.

So I told Peppers the gist of the mission: That Saddam was "probably" taking taxis from hiding place to hiding place. That he could recruit three of the best paparazzi in Hollywood to find Saddam. Then, after a two-week crash training course in CIA tradecraft, he and his team would have two months to find Saddam. I told him that they'd all be working undercover as journalists for *Northern Exposure*, a fictional Canadian newsmagazine. That they would photograph and tail taxi drivers and their passengers, which hopefully would lead us to Saddam.

"How many taxis are there in Iraq?" Peppers asked me.

I should have known the answer, but I didn't. So I did what every CIA officer must do well: I lied. I told him "a few hundred," adding that half of them were probably in Shiite-dominated southern Iraq, where Hussein, a Sunni, would never go anyway.

I didn't think it would be a problem. I didn't think he'd back out. I miscalculated. I knew that Dr. Rice was *not* going to be happy.

TOM PEPPERS

Hollywood Bureau Chief, *Them! Weekly*

They had me by the balls. I didn't want my wife to know about the London sex tape. So what do they do? The douche bags go and blackmail me by leaking that sex tape to *Them!*. Fine, he got me fair and square.

I actually was prepared to sign the agreement when I met him out in the desert, but on the way there I found out about the sex tape. Millions had seen my skinny white ass next to London Marriott's skinny white ass. Worst of all, my wife Jessica now was talking to the press; she'd given an interview to *Them!* My supposed ally Bobby Lesser turns out to be Bobby the back stabber! Yeah, with five exclamation points!!!!! Suddenly, I had become one of the stars, one of *them*!

Then Posner has the balls to tell me he basically has no idea where Saddam's hiding, that I'm this sorry-ass administration's last hope at finding the guy. That's why I busted out of there.

Five MP's on one knee greeted me at the exit gate, pointing their 9-mm Berettas at me. Five red lasers focused dead-center on my chest.

Then my cell phone rang. It was Barry.

"Look, it wasn't my idea to leak the video," he says in a panic. "It was Dr. Rice's."

"Why'd she go and do something stupid like that?"

"I don't know," he replied. "I guess she wanted to make sure you wouldn't change your mind. Ms. Rice doesn't like to leave things to chance."

"She's a bitch, is what she is."

"But she also has a lot of respect for you," he said, suddenly not sounding smug. "And, as hard as it is for me to admit this, so do I."

I didn't believe the liar for a second.

I countered, "Then why do you do nothing but put me down?"

"Honestly?" he said.

"Yeah," I said, "a little honesty would be nice for a change."

"I'm jealous of you."

"Of me?"

"Yeah, of your freedom. There's something very American about what you do. You tell the truth about public figures, no matter how damaging it might be to them. Truth is, I respect what you do."

"Well, Barry, you have a weird way of showing your affection for people."

"I'll admit that. Deep down, I am envious of you. Everyone knows your successes, but I work in obscurity. If I foil an assassination plot, or turn a foreigner into a spy, the public doesn't know about it, let alone know that I was the one who did it. Working for the CIA is a thankless job, Tom."

"Then why do you do it?"

"I've been asking myself the same question lately."

Barry looked damn pitiful, as if he'd just been told that Dockers had gone out of style.

"It's all spin these days, Tom," he added. "I got into the intelligence game because I wanted our country's leaders to have all the facts in order to make the best decisions."

"There's no such thing as facts anymore," I said. "I should know, I'm a journalist."

"Yeah, I know," Barry said. "You think Jayson Blair could weave a tale? You should see how much this administration distorts the facts."

I almost would have felt sorry for the guy had he not just spent the last week lying straight to my face, wrecking my marriage or ruining my reputation. But I was willing to give him the benefit of the doubt. In Hollywood, we love comebacks.

Not only was Barry admitting that he respected what I do, but he was begging me to do this job. That meant I was in the perfect position to get the only thing we in Hollywood really want: money.

Before I went in for the kill, however, Barry, whom I could see standing a hundred yards behind me in my rear-view mirror, continued his blathering, and I used the secret weapon of every good interviewer: I pretended to listen.

He said, "Look, we both know you'd rather be back in Hollywood finding celebrities eating at the Ivy, but the bottom line is that you've committed to do this. We're in this together, and if you help us capture Saddam, you'll be an American hero."

"I don't want to be a hero," I said firmly (and honestly).

"Then what do you want?"

"To be rich beyond belief. I want the reward."

"What reward?"

"Don't play stupid, Barry. You know damn well about the $25 million reward you guys are offering anyone with information directly leading to Saddam's capture."

"Oh," he exhaled. "That reward."

"Yeah, *that* one. It's not just because I'm greedy. There's no way I'll convince three paparazzi to join me without the promise of a big payoff. These sharks are used to making six-figures a shot."

"Okay," Barry says. "Hold on."

* * *

POSNER: Dr. Rice, sorry to bother you, but it's Barry. I'm out at Area 99 and I have Mr. Peppers on the other line. He stormed out of our meeting as soon as I told him about the mission details. He claims he won't do it unless he and his team can get the reward money.

RICE: Does he realize that if he doesn't help us we will leak all our intelligence on him? I mean, the Lindsey Bohan incident alone could land him in prison for statutory rape.

POSNER: He doesn't care.

RICE: Oh, goshdarnit, Barry. Hold on. Let me conference in the President.

(Phone rings nine times)

BUSH: Y'ello.

RICE: Sir, I'm sorry to bug you on a Sunday, but –

BUSH: Damnit. Can't a guy get a weekend off for once?

RICE: Sorry, sir, but we've got a situation here. Mr. Peppers is threatening not to participate in Operation Hollywood if we don't offer him the reward money.

BUSH: Doh!

RICE: Sir?

BUSH: Holy moly! Did you see that?

RICE: See what?

BUSH: *Access Hollywood.* Nancy O'Dell just interviewed London Marriott, and the gal said I was her favorite president of all time. Isn't she just a cutie?

RICE: Sir, can we return the discussion back to the Peppers situation?

BUSH: Sure, give him the money--but only if he finds that butcher.

RICE: But, sir, who will we tell Congress we paid? They're going to want to know to whom we issued the reward. They'll want documentation and so forth.

BUSH: Worry about that land mine when we cross it.

RICE: And if the land mine blows up?

BUSH: Listen, Condi, stop killing my buzz. I gotta run now. My weasely nephew Billy Bush is interviewing J. Lo! Bushie out.

RICE: You heard him, Barry. Just tell Peppers that the money is his if he achieves the objective.

POSNER: But we can't promise him anything if Congress stops us from –

RICE: Just do it, Mr. Posner. You still want that promotion, don't you?

POSNER: Yes, ma'am. Of course, I do.

RICE: Do everything right on this project and you'll be deputy to the National Security Adviser.

POSNER: Copy that.

TOM PEPPERS

Bureau Chief, Operation Hollywood

Fabloid Editor Rule #3: Never accept their first offer.

Fabloid Editor Rule #4: Always get the most money you can squeeze out of them.

Fabloid Editor Rule #5: Laugh all the way to the Bentley dealer.

In reality, the mission wasn't going to be that hard. Luckily, Posner didn't know that I'd done far more with far less intelligence. One time, in fact, I got a tip that Bruce Willis was on "tropical vacation" with a mystery blond. Two days later, I had a team of paps snapping him skinny-dipping with Brooke Burke in Costa Rica. Fabloid gold, baby.

I knew those government hacks would cave. They're in the public sector for a reason; they'd get eaten alive in the real world. I'd already gotten Jaimee on board; she was the hardest-working, most loyal shooter in town. Now all I needed were two more skilled shooters. And I only wanted the best. Unfortunately, the best photographers aren't necessarily the best human beings. That explains how Jordie Black became part of the team.

JORDIE BLACK

Photographer, Black Bronco Photos

I'm not going to lie to you, dude. Tom Peppers knows a lot about the animal of celebrity. It's like he has a Celebrity Sixth Sense. He can find anyone famous, pretty much anywhere, at anytime. And it's like the more they don't want to be found, the better he is at finding them. He's got the best sources in the business and has the uncanny ability to know the enemy.

Tom's the best intelligence gatherer in town. Tom knows when something's going to happen before it even happens, and that's valuable in a profession in which timing is almost everything. But if there's one thing the guy can't do it is take a fucking picture. That's why he needed us more than we needed him. And did I mention that I absolutely hated his guts?

TOM PEPPERS

Bureau Chief, Operation Hollywood

Yeah, you might say that me and Jordie shared a little history before this operation. But, as far as I'm concerned, that was all it was: history—of the ancient variety.

Look, Jessica was a big girl and made her own decisions. Was it my fault that she dumped his ass for mine? Was it my fault she found me more attractive? Is it my fault she wanted to get married and Jordie didn't? Sour grapes, is what he is.

Don't get me wrong. Jordie is a very good paparazzo. I won't shit you on that. The guy always gets his picture—always. I respect him for that, and I'll give him his props. But business is business, and everything else is just that: everything else. I decided that if he could focus on achieving our objective, I'd take him with us. If he couldn't be a grown-up, then he could stay back and watch us take the most important pictures in the history of military intelligence, not to mention American journalism. The ball was in his court.

JORDIE BLACK

Photographer, Black Bronco Photos

Here's an example of what kind of guy Tom Peppers is. A couple summers ago, he calls me and says, "Jordie, Matt Leblanc is getting married in Hawaii in two weeks. But he and his fiancée are already there. Can you go and cover?"

One thing you should know about me is that I never turn down a chance to shoot a wedding. The chicks who read the slicks love weddings, and if they love them then the slicks love them, which means the slicks will pay top dollar for wedding photos. And if *Them!* is going to pay my expenses to fly to paradise for a few weeks, I'm game. So I went. I figured Tom was a good guy—you know, for giving me a great assignment, what was basically a $200,000 gift.

What I didn't know at the time was that a few hours earlier he had just assigned my then-girlfriend, Jessica, who was a freelance reporter for Tom, to a week-long stakeout up at Neverland, meaning I couldn't bring her with me. It wasn't the end of the world. We'd been dating for over a year and Jessica and I had been apart for several weeks before. No big deal.

But check out what happens. In Hawaii, I get the pictures of a lifetime: Matt Leblanc walking the aisle, the bride tossing the bouquet, Jennifer Aniston dancing with Lisa Kudrow, the full celebrity-wedding monty. It was the greatest day of my career. Problem is, the next day I get back to L.A. and there's this message on my answering machine from Jessica: "We're done, surfer boy. I'm with Tom now. Don't ever call me again." And that was it, just like that. It felt like a punch in the gut. Still does.

So this goes a long way to saying that if it weren't for that snake Tom Peppers Jessica and I would still have been a couple. I really believed that. The only reason I could even think to stomach working with Tom is that Jessica had dumped him, and I hoped she'd come back to her senses and realize the mistake she'd made and come back to me. As I saw things: Jessica was J. Lo, Tom Peppers was Ben Affleck, and I was Cris Judd—the good guy she should never have left in the first place.

TOM PEPPERS

Bureau Chief, Operation Hollywood

I am guilty of a lot of things, but I did not steal Jordie Black's girlfriend. I didn't take Jessica from anyone. He lost her.

I was on a stakeout outside Neverland for a week in the middle of nowhere. We were putting in eighteen-hour days, waiting for Michael to come out and head to the plastic surgeon (a nurse had tipped us off that he was getting a new nose stitched on). The entire time all Jessica could do is complain about how Jordie is self-centered, how all he wants to do is take pictures, surf and, when he's not doing either just lay around and have quick-and-dirty sex. And I mean dirty. I guess the guy has a porn collection (filled with nasty shit with animals and whatnot) that is so big it dwarfs the Smithsonian. Safe to say, Jessica was an unhappy girl, and I was a single, happy guy. It was pure nature, just meant to happen. Opposites attract.

You've gotta remember, Jessica is a beautiful girl. The long blonde hair that danced on her shoulders, the alabaster skin, the hazel eyes, that anatomically correct hip-to-waist ratio. And those lips, so full and red and puffy. Holy smokes. I mean, she's Hollywood-hot. If she didn't have a slight lisp, she'd probably be a movie star instead of a journalist. But I find even her imperfections irresistible.

So when Jessica asked me what I thought of Jordie, I told her the truth: he was too immature, too young, and that she deserved an older, more sensitive, more loving, more financially stable boyfriend. Of course, I was talking about myself.

JORDIE BLACK

Photographer, Black Bronco Photos

News flash: I'm not over Jessica. Yeah, that breakup still stings like a jelly fish, dude. I had to read about her marriage to Tom in the *New York Post*, and I wanted to kill myself. It's not as bad as it used to be. I would sit on stakeouts and spend like fourteen hours just obsessing about how I would win her back. On weekends, I would surf, hoping the waves would help me forget her. But no matter how hard I tried I just couldn't get Jessica out of my mind. She really got under my skin unlike any other girl. Even still, to this day I can't go by her old place on Ocean Avenue without looking for her Saab convertible parked in front. Girls like Jessica are dangerous. There is an inherent downside to dating such a sexy girl, and it's that they can be as cruel as they are hot. You don't get something for nothing. Whenever I think of her, my stomach still gets tied in knots. I can't even watch porn anymore because every naked girl I see reminds me of her. That's how much it hurts, dude. It really hurts.

And I'll never forgive that douche bag for stealing her. Tom Peppers isn't the nice guy he wants you to think he is. Tom's the master of propaganda. He can spin any facts into any story he wants. It might be brilliant when you're writing celebrity trash, but when it comes to real life it can ruin lives. I'm living proof.

I know a thing or two about propaganda. I was a political science major at UCLA and wrote my senior thesis on Soviet Propaganda. The Soviet regime was the first modern regime to understand that the public's perception was their reality. They knew the key to controlling perception was controlling the media. If the leaders sensed the public thought Leonid Breznev was growing unpopular, they'd stage photo-ops showing him being cheered on by hundreds of supporters at a staged rally. Of course, what you didn't see were the sharp-shooters just off-camera ready to mow down anyone who didn't cheer loud enough. Then, of course, the Soviets perfected what became known as the "parade trick." At military parades in Red Square, the Soviets would create the illusion that they had ten times the weapons that they really had by running the same bombers, tanks and missiles around the block several times. It worked. Tricks like that scared President Reagan into building up the biggest weapons arsenal in the history of mankind.

But my goal out of college was to move to Washington and get into political consulting. Problem is, I never graduated. When my dad died (of being a drunk), my mom couldn't afford to send me back for my last two years. So I had to give up my dream of doing something that truly matters socially. I so resented that my family couldn't afford to pay for school that I vowed that I would be rich some day so my kids wouldn't have to suffer. Noble, huh?

That's when I started chasing celebrities. I got my start as an autograph collector. I'd stand outside an actor's hotel, and when he came out I'd ambush him with a rack of photos. I'd get up to fifty bucks an autograph. With every arrogant stroke of the celebrity's pen I would see dollar signs. Initially, I hoped the autographs would net me enough money to eventually afford finishing college.

Then one day outside the Starbucks in Malibu, as Tommy Lee signed photo after photo for me, I looked across the street and saw this old dude with a pony-tail sitting in his SUV. He was taking pictures with the longest telephoto lens I'd ever seen. I mean, the thing had to be three feet long. So when Tommy left, I walked up to the guy and asked him how much he'd get for the photos he'd just taken.

"Probably about ten thousand bucks," he said. "And that's just in North America. It's double that overseas."

Meanwhile, I'd just made a measly two-hundred bucks.

"I wish I could take photos," I whined.

"You can," the old guy said. "Being a paparazzo is ninety percent CIA agent, and ten percent photographer. You obviously know how to track down stars. I can teach you the photography part."

That was the last day I asked a celebrity for an autograph.

The guy in the SUV gave me his card. His name was Bronco. Three years later, I was one of the highest-paid celebrity photographers in the business, and Bronco was my business partner. Our photo agency was called Black Bronco. We kicked everyone's asses.

We divided the work to fit our styles and strengths. I'd shoot most of the tough jobs—the stakeouts, the late-night flashes outside the clubs, the out-of-towners—and chase around the younger stars, the Justin Timberlakes, Reese Witherspoons, the Paris Hiltons. Meanwhile Bronco did a lot of the car work and most of the geriatric stars like Barbara Streisand. I was happier being a celebrity photographer than my former dream of being a policy troll in Washington. Most important, I knew that someday I would be rich as fuck. I was a content guy. Then Jessica broke my heart.

JESSICA PEPPERS

Tom Peppers's Hot Wife

The truth is that neither Tom nor Jordie is the perfect man for me. Like any guys, they both have their plusses and minuses. Before I left Jordie for Tom, I made a checklist. Girls do that. It helps us clear the emotional clouds so we can see things more logically.

When I was with Jordie, it was a transitional time in my life. I was twenty-five, and I felt like I was a quarter of the way through my life and needed to assess everything. I wanted to decide what kind of man I should be with for the rest of my life. So, anyway, I made this check-list thingy.

	TOM	**JORDIE**
SEX		**X**
MONEY	**X**	
BRAINS	**X**	
MATURITY	**X**	
LOOKS		**X**
FAME	**X**	

As you can see, Tom had the whole package. Well, not exactly. He is, you know, hung like a hamster. But, still, Tom offered a lot more overall than did Jordie, who, while being Brad-Pitt hot and a champion in the sack, possessed all the maturity of Lindsay Lohan.

At the time I met Tom I was working as a reporter for him, and, as they say, power can be a real aphrodisiac. I normally hate to be bossed around and told what to do, but Tom was so charming that he made me feel like he was doing me a favor by letting me work for him. I think it's that same manipulative power that makes him a good interviewer. He can get someone to say what they don't want to say just by making them feel like they owe it to him to be honest. I've always respected that quality in him.

After we started dating, whenever he got mad at me at work, we'd always come home and, well, have great makeup sex. What

Tom lacked in muscle tone, sexual performance and raw good looks he made up for with confidence and status around town. They say L.A. girls are high-maintenance, but it's not like we're a bunch of little Paris Hiltons running around in our designer clothes and "perma-waxed" bodies. Some of us care about more stuff than just our looks.

I know it sounds really retarded, but I'd always wanted to be an actress. That was pretty much my only goal when I got out of high school. That's why for my high school graduation present my parents got me a ten-thousand-dollar boob job. Dad got me the left, and Mom the right. Isn't that so cool? I realize this might sound weird to you, but I grew up in Palos Verdes, where being flat as a surfboard is considered more shameful than being a coke addict. I am not kidding. And if I was going to make it in Hollywood, I needed to add something up top. Seriously. Like, it's just reality, you know?

With my new boobs, innocent looks, and my parents' money to burn on acting lessons (and clothes!), I got myself an agent and began the long, painful process that is being an aspiring actress in Hollywood. I'd go on auditions for this and that but then never get the part. I couldn't even get the part of "Girlfriend in Car" for a Snickers commercial. It was brutal. After about two years of dealing with all the crap, I wanted out.

Looking around, I saw women in their thirties who were still struggling to get that breakthrough role, but who were already too long in the tooth by Hollywood standards. I didn't want to be washed-up at thirty—when the crow's feet come and the biological clock ticks louder and louder.

Although I had had enough with acting, I was still addicted to celebrity. And I decided that if I could no longer be a celebrity I wanted at least to be around them.

Us and *Them*! were always my favorite magazines. I'd read them front to back every week, studying everything the actresses were wearing and doing, as if it were my Bible and stuff. Every day I'd go on gossipgirl.com and chat on the message boards about what was going on with them.

At night, I'd go to clubs like Skybar on the hot nights just so I could meet, or even just hang around, famous and/or powerful guys. The Hollywood social scene is so Darwinian. It's both awesome and disgusting at the same time. I mean, this town has no pretensions. It is what it is: all about looking good. Back in the day, I'd get all dolled up in a mini-skirt, tight top and heels, my makeup heavy enough to say "slut" yet light enough not to say "hooker." Every night was like competing in a beauty pageant, because, if—the horror! — I didn't look sexy enough on the sidewalk in front the club, the doorman wouldn't let me in. And if I didn't get in, that meant I wouldn't meet that one slime-ball producer or casting agent who could get me a role.

I'm aware that a lot of people think this is all very shallow and gross and judgmental and just an all-around wretched culture to choose to live in. But, for that time in my life, I loved it. Because A) I was good at it, and B) If I wanted to win the game, I had to play the game.

Now, did I want to be out clubbing with a bunch of X-dropping club kids when I was thirty? No way. Did I want to have my career success be determined by a bunch of sexist producers who cared way more about my ass than my acting? No. But who was it that once said, "Know thyself?" I can't remember. But it was someone really smart. And I was smart enough to know this about myself, that my two favorite things in the whole world were sex and celebrity.

So, one day while sitting in a bikini by the pool at the Chateau Marmont reading *Them!,* as Tobey and Leo feasted their disgusting little eyes on my body from across the patio, I had a ... what do you call it? I had, um, an epiphany! Yeah, that's it. An epiphany. I realized that the reason I loved the celebrity magazines so much was that the best ones—basically, *Us Weekly* and *Them! Weekly*—were so delicious because just about everything they have in them is about sex and celebrity. Seriously, just look at some covers and you will see that's what the magazines are selling. How Jessica Simpson Keeps Nick Happy ... Did J. Lo Cheat on Ben ... Hollywood's Hottest Hunks ... Sexiest Man Alive ... Sexy or Surgery? ... Fifty Most Beautiful. ... Sure, every now and then *People* will put on some heart-tugging human interest story, but the real celebrity magazines—*Us, Them!, InTouch, Star*—are all about what Tom always calls "Sexlebrity." Tom is so smart.

Literally a few hours after that light bulb popped on in my head, I squeezed into a pair of jeans, sneakers and a white Gap shirt. No mini-skirts tonight. I pulled my hair back in a pony tail, stuffed a notebook in my purse, and put on just a little bit of lipstick. And then I got in my Jetta and drove across town to the Lounge in West Hollywood.

It was a Thursday night, which meant that by midnight every

hot, young star would be drinking and dancing and flirting inside: Leo, Justin, Tobey, Colin, Ashton, Britney, Christina—you name it. And, as was the routine, a half dozen paparazzi (all guys, except for a disgusting old fat lady) were standing on the sidewalk across from the velvet rope, which penned in the mini-skirted masses like they were a herd of really good-looking cattle.

The first photographer I saw shooting the hotties was a hottie himself. All the other photographers were, first of all, ugly, not to mention either Eurotrash with ugly shoes or, not to be racist or anything, Mexicans wearing baseball caps turned backwards. But this one guy had sandy-blond hair that he either didn't comb or combed so expertly that it didn't look like he'd even touched it. He wore hundred-dollar jeans that fit loose around his hips but tight around his ass. He was well over six feet tall, had the sexy jaw-line of Brad Pitt and a build like JFK Jr. Totally my kind of guy.

"Hi," I said to him peppily, extending a hand to shake. "I'm Jessica, and I want to be a paparazzi."

He looked over at me, scanned me up and down, chuckled and replied, "And you are whose publicist?"

"No one's," I said. "I want to be a celebrity photographer."

"Okay," he said, putting his camera down and letting it dangle around his neck. So sexy. "Then let me ask you this: Have you ever taken a picture with anything but an automatic camera?"

"No," I replied, eagerly adding, "but I really, really want to learn how to take real pictures."

"Honey," he said, "I hate to break this news to you, but there ain't no girl paparazzi. This is a man's job. What you want to be is a reporter. Chicks do the reporting. They interview these idiots. Guys take the pictures."

Suddenly, the paparazzi started flashing their bulbs. Justin Timberlake had arrived and my dreamboat photographer had work to do. A trashy blonde (who was NOT Britney) clutched Justin's arm as he walked toward the entrance. The flashbulbs were popping like the red carpet of the Academy Awards. "Go ask that new girl what her name is!" my hottie photographer-friend shouted my way without taking his eyes off his targets.

As Justin was about to take the girl inside by her hand, I grabbed her arm. She twisted her neck back at me and our blue eyes locked. "I'm sorry, but what's your name?" And, before being yanked inside, she said, "Jenna Dewan."

The flash storm subsided when Justin ducked inside the club.

"So what's her name?" the photographer asked.

"Jenna Dewan," I said.

"Awesome," he said. "That means he has finally dumped Britney, and now he's banging one of his backup dancers."

"Why's that awesome?"

"Because your information just tripled the value of my picture," he said, finally smiling. "Good job."

"Cool," I said, my first words as a freshly minted celebrity journalist. "Now tell me, what's your name?"

"Jordie."

And just like that not only had I found a new career, but I had found a new boyfriend, even if he had a name like a girl.

TOM PEPPERS

Bureau Chief, Operation Hollywood

Life would be boring without challenges. And I couldn't think of anything more challenging than hunting down Saddam Hussein. When I was in graduate school at Columbia, I had a feeling that someday I would do something great, that I'd be part of a journalistic project that would make history. The mere thought of it kept me up late at night. I'd sit in my dank windowless box of an apartment on the Upper West Side scheming of different ways to make my mark in the pantheon of American journalism.

One night, in between watching a cockroach nibble the crumbs off my hot plate, I got to thinking about all the black-and-white POW-MIA stickers, flags and t-shirts that I was seeing all the time. This was the early '90s, mind you, when a lot of paranoid Vietnam vets still thought there could be hundreds of American soldiers imprisoned in the dense jungles. Back then, I didn't even own a computer; rather, I'd write everything down on legal pads and then type it into a computer in the lab up in the journalism building. That night, I began furiously scribbling a grant proposal for what I passionately felt would be my Big Project. I wanted to fly to Vietnam and investigate the villages and jungles of North Vietnam with a translator, one by one determining the status of the some three hundred men who the government had still classified as Missing In Action. I wanted to submit the proposal to the journalism think thank the Freedom Forum, which I hoped would issue me a ten-thousand-dollar grant to work on the project I had dubbed, "The Search for Truth."

A month later, the president of the think tank called me into his Manhattan office for an interview. I was so nervous.

The guy's name was Dennis McDaniel, a fat, crotchety, bow-tied, and profoundly smug former foreign editor of the *New York Times* who, even in his seventies, had not lost his idiot-sounding Alabama accent. Meanwhile, being twenty-three and having worked zero days as a professional journalist, I was as green as corn in May.

"So, Tom," I perfectly remember him saying, "what makes you think you're so qualified to find the truth about the POW-MIA issue? I mean, some of the world's greatest journalists have written about this issue for the last twenty years. Don't you think it's a tad unrealistic that you will get to the bottom of this issue?"

"Well, sir, I can understand why you'd think that the truth will be so hard to — "

Mr. Southern Santa Claus interrupted me with a belly laugh. "The truth? What do you know about the truth?"

"That's just it," I replied. "I don't know what is the truth. That's why I want to go and find out."

The red-faced oldster stared across his oak desk at me, squinted through his hockey-puck-thick bifocals, and exhaled as if he was about reveal the DaVinci code. "Son, journalists can only report the facts, not the truth. Son, *truth* is only the version of the facts that people choose to believe."

At that moment, I took his comment as nothing but a cynical statement coming from a crusty old journalism burnout. And when I didn't get the grant, I figured the idiot just didn't get it. But, after having battled through the spin to get the facts in the Hollywood Industrial complex, and having worked as a tool for the CIA in the hunt for Saddam, I now appreciate what the fat bastard was trying to say. I wish I would have listened back then, because it would have saved me a lot of needless headaches over the years. But profundity, like peak male sexual performance, is wasted on the young.

BRONCO

Photographer, Black Bronco Photos

The Brits call us "snappers" or "paps." The Americans have more respectfully called us "photographers" or "paparazzi." Recently, though, a disturbing term has entered the lexicon: "stalkerazzi." Personally, I hate the word. It suggests that what we do is somehow illegal or wrong or unethical. I find it offensive.

I've never understood how renting studio space, hiring a team of stylists and makeup artists and then pressing a button on a camera makes someone a professional photographer, yet what we street photographers do is unprofessional. I capture images of stars in their natural habitat—at the beach, on set, at the coffee shop, the gym, the Botox doctor. And for the last twenty years, I have been paid to do this. That makes me a professional.

Some of the new, young, hot-dog paparazzi give the rest of us pros a bad name. There's a lot of guys out there who will do anything to get a picture. They'll have a second driver pull in front of a star and cause an accident just to get a photo of them in a car wreck. They'll sneak onto private property and take pictures of Jennifer Aniston sunbathing topless in her back yard. They'll taunt drunk stars in order to get the "angry-celeb" shot. These slime balls give the rest of us ethical paparazzi a bad name. We're no different than lawyers. There are good ones defending the little guy, and then there are the ambulance chasers with no soul.

Sadly, the game has changed since when I started back in the early '80s, when there were maybe a dozen professional paparazzi in L.A. who took candid shots of stars. We'd stand outside places like Chasen's and Morton's and snap them coming and going. We'd photograph actors working on movie sets. More often than not, publicists, agents and managers who wanted photos of their clients out there tipped us off. Often, the actors would call us themselves. Nowadays, we have Cameron Diaz flipping us the bird and Gwyneth Paltrow pulling a hood over her head. And the only time we hear from someone in an actor's camp is when a lawyer writes us a cease-and-desist letter.

The competition is fierce. There are so many guys snapping around town, all of them chasing the same few dozen stars whose images fetch big-time money. I don't even bother parking across from the Ivy anymore; there are so many guys there already that any pics I get are virtually worthless when I try to sell them to the slicks.

Gentlemen photographers are a dying breed. To survive in today's paparazzi market, you need to be a dirtbag. Or at least work with one. That's why I've partnered with Jordie. He's young and hungry and aggressive and totally willing to do anything to get a shot—lie, trespass, speed, park in handicapped spots, verbally harass and provoke. And it doesn't hurt that all the female stars think he's cute and always stop and pose a full-body shot.

The game has changed. I'm forty-six years old—ancient in this business. I've come to that point in my life where I've started to wonder what's next, whether I should be doing something more meaningful with my life.

I started out wanting to be a war photographer. The first photographic images I remember seeing as a kid were from the Vietnam War. That soldier pointing a pistol to the temple of that poor Vietnamese. That was a paparazzi shot, only the subjects were made famous after the shot, not before. I applied to the army, but I didn't pass the physical. I didn't pass the eye exam, ironically enough.

My first job in photojournalism was as an intern at the Associated Press bureau in Los Angeles. I only had an associate's degree, since my parents couldn't afford to send me to college. They wouldn't hire me because I didn't have a bachelor's. That's my sob story.

I ended up getting a staff photographer job for the *Malibu Times,* where I was working when I accidentally took my first paparazzi shot. In 1982, I sold a picture of Johnny Carson playing tennis to *People* magazine and got $1,500 for it. Since I was making that much a month at the paper, it wasn't long before I was spending all my free time photographing celebrities.

Twenty years later, I was ready for a new challenge. So when Tom approached me with this Iraq assignment, I had to take it seriously. In a way, I'm going back to what I wanted to do in the first place: shoot war. And when Tom told me the money would be so good that I could retire when the assignment was over, the decision to join him was easy.

I've never had a wife or kids. Papping has been my wife, girlfriend, and my mistress. I know, it's sort of sad. The last time I had sex was ... I'd rather not say, it's been such an embarrassingly long time. All I have to say that Jordie's the closest thing I've ever had to a son. That's why I call him "my boy." And what Bronco does, so does my boy.

THE OVAL OFFICE

24 October 2004

8:30 a.m.

(Donald Rumsfeld, Colin Powell, Karl Rove and Dick Cheney enter together as Bush surfs the Internet on his laptop.)

BUSH: Whatchy'all doin' this mornin'?

RUMSFELD: Unfortunately, we have to report we're not doing very well, sir. We need to discuss some issues with you.

BUSH: Shoot.

CHENEY: Mr. President, it's about the WMD's.

BUSH: The whats?

CHENEY: The Weapons of Mass Destruction, sir. The nuclear devices and weapons technology that Tenet and CIA had led us to believe Saddam was developing.

BUSH: Oh, yeah, those nucular weapons. So what about those WD's?

CHENEY: WMD's.

BUSH: Okay, what about the whatever-you-call-'ems?

CHENEY: Uh, sir, there are none.

BUSH: Great! That is great ... ain't it? WMD's are a bad thing, after all.

ROVE: No, sir, it's *not* great. In point of fact, it's a serious political problem for this administration.

BUSH: Why's that?

ROVE: Mr. President, in the speeches we wrote for you last year the main reason we cited as cause to declare war was because Saddam possessed WMD's. But for the last seven months, we've looked in every bunker, every warehouse, every hole in the ground, and we have found zero evidence of such weapons.

RUMSFELD: Zilch, zero, nada.

CHENEY: Sir, all we've found are grenades and some Soviet-era missiles and porn stash in Saddam's palace.

RUMSFELD: I have to say, Tenet really dropped the ball on this one, Mr. President. The entire war was based on faulty intelligence. Now we have a substantial political and diplomatic challenge on our hands. Wait till those commie bastards at *60 Minutes* hear about this one.

ROVE: We're fucked.

CHENEY: Uh, sir, I'd have to agree with Karl on that.

BUSH: You guys are really killing my coffee buzz. Whatever happened to those prisoners we've been interrogating in Abu Ghraib? Rummy, you said if we humiliated them enough they'd start singin' like canaries. You tellin' me none of those sand-suckers knows where these weapons are being hidden? What gives, buddy?

RUMSFELD: It's my position that we need to get tougher on these prisoners. We're thinking of taking the intimidation to the next level: stripping them naked and taking pictures. In college, we called it hazing. We must crack these Muslims.

POWELL: You've got to be kidding me! This is the worst idea I have heard since Don drafted an Iraqi war plan but no plan for governance after the invasion. Don, you should be ashamed of yourself.

BUSH: Whatever. Just make sure we abuse and humiliate them in a very Christian way.

POWELL: But, sir, might I suggest that –

BUSH: Pipe down, Colin! Can't ya see I'm trying to *think* here, trying to *solve* problems for America. Just let me think about this issue for a sec, put my mind on the problems at hand for America.

(Powell, Cheney, Rumsfeld and Rove sit silently for four minutes as the President gazes out at the Rose Garden.)

BUSH: That's it! I got it. Okay, couldn't we just do the old plant trick?

CHENEY: I don't understand, sir. The *what* trick?

BUSH: You know, we could plant some nucular material over there and say we found it. That sorta thing.

ROVE: We *could* do that. We definitely could that.

CHENEY: No, we could *not*! That would not be right.

POWELL: I couldn't support that, Mr. President. We can't defraud the American people any more than we have already.

CHENEY: Believe it or not, I actually agree with Colin. I would have to tender my resignation and go back to my cushy oil job back at Halliburton.

RUMSFELD: I'd have to agree with these guys on this one. And, sir, if I might add, your father would never do such a thing.

BUSH: Now why you go bringin' my daddy into this? That ain't fair, Rummy. Ain't right at all. Just thinkin' out loud. Don't persecute me. Makin' me feel like Jesus on the cross over here. You're not gonna tell Daddy I said that, are you?

RUMSFELD: No. But, George, we can't even think of planting weapons. That cretin Bob Woodward would nail us on that one.

ROVE: If we pulled it off, it would be political genius, however. I'll do a poll on it.

CHENEY: Do you not have *any* principles, Karl?

BUSH: Hey, simmer down, Dickie. No need to tear the bark off Rover. Just doin' his job, givin' me *options* to these problems.

ROVE: And, thanks to this WMD's mess, we do have serious problems—at home and abroad.

CHENEY: That's the problem around here, Mr. President. Everyone wants to give you options, but no one has any answers. Colin is the worst offender. He'll give you options all day long. Sir, with all due respect, I'm giving you answers—at home and abroad.

BUSH: Hey, speaking of broad. I gotta let you guys in on somethin'. Condi ain't around is she? Good. Check this out, boys.

(Bush turns his laptop around and shows them an image of a bikini-clad London Marriott.)

CHENEY: Who's that, er, rather attractive young lady?

RUMSFELD: I believe that's Britney Spears.

ROVE: No, Don, that is Jessica Simpson.

BUSH: Nope, you are both wrong. Take a guess, Colin.

POWELL: I don't know. Maybe Jenna Jameson.

BUSH: Nope. You're all wrong. Dickie?

CHENEY: Christina Aguilera?

BUSH: No, boys. This here is our very own weapon of mass destruction!

LONDON MARRIOTT

White House Press Secretary

I don't know. Since I was a little girl, I'd always wanted to be a secretary. The cute little skirts, the serious-girl glasses, the dress shirts unbuttoned at the top showing cleavage and stuff like that. I mean, like, Business Barbie was my favorite doll.

I had the feeling that working as a press secretary was going to be a pretty awesome experience, obviously from the fashion perspective of things. Like, this job was definitely a dream come true. America is the greatest country in the world for so many reasons, but, for me, the thing that makes it way-cool is that, besides the awesome shopping, you can be rich and beautiful and famous yet still find success in life. It's so trippy.

TOM PEPPERS

Bureau Chief, Operation Hollywood

Bronco, by the way, is just his paparazzi name. His real name is Jose Martinez, which is the name he worked under for the first ten years of his career as a straight photographer. But then came the O.J. Simpson case and that's when he became Bronco.

As the story goes, the second he heard that O.J.'s ex-wife had been murdered, Jose parked outside O.J.'s estate in Brentwood. For days, he waited for the Juice to come out, and when the White Bronco finally pulled out one afternoon, Jose followed it.

O.J. wasn't driving, mind you. His friend Al Cowling was, but the money shot was to be had in the back seat, where O.J. lay holding a pistol to his head.

A few minutes later, Jose pulls next to the White Bronco as it's sitting at a red light at Bundy and San Vicente Boulevard. Jose jumps out of his car and snaps a picture of O.J. cowering in the back seat—pistol and all. It was the only photo taken of O.J. in the White Bronco. That photo turned struggling paparazzo Jose Martinez into the game's hottest photog. And it made him rich.

Other paps starting calling him Bronco, and, well, it just sort of stuck. I was the first to admit that Bronco was an old bastard, some might say too old for an undercover operation in a hostile setting. But I felt it in my gut that, with Bronco, all things were possible. Plus, let's face it, Bronco is the only person Jordie Black will listen to. And I needed Jordie.

BRONCO

Photographer, Black Bronco Photos

Every pap worth his salt keeps a box in his car containing all the equipment he needs. We call it a toy box. And they say I have the best toy box in the business. But since all my gear costs about $50,000, it's also the most expensive box in the business.

I don't tell anyone what's in my box. It's just something you don't talk about. It's no one's business but mine. If other paps find out what goodies I use, they'd copy me. In a competitive business like celebrity photography, you need every edge you can get. Even Jordie has never seen everything in my toy box.

JORDIE BLACK

Photographer, Black Bronco Photos

A lot of old-school paps think equipment makes the photographer. Well, it doesn't, bro'. Give me an eight-dollar Kodak point-and-shoot from Rite-Aid and J.B. will shoot anyone in any situation—guaranteed. It's not the camera; it's the man behind the camera. So I don't mind telling you what's in my box.

First of all, J.B.'s a Canon guy. Most paps either use Nikon or Canon. It's sort of like BMW or Mercedes. They're both excellent products, so it's merely a matter of taste. Canon tends to be more user-friendly, and when you're out in the field and have three seconds to point and shoot you can't afford to the let the equipment get in the way. To be safe, I always carry two digital Canon EOS bodies with me. My Canons are fast; they shoot 2.5 frames-per-second. Real paparazzi haven't used a non-digital camera since 2000. These days, you gotta shoot digital. It's just as high a quality as film and you can transmit instantly from your laptop to the slicks. In the old days before digital, a pap would get his shots, then run to a lab to process the film, then look at the negatives through an eye-piece, then scan the photos he wanted to transmit, then transmit them. I get exhausted just thinkin' about it, 'bro. The whole process could take five hours. Nowadays, it takes about five seconds to do all that right off your laptop.

There's a lot of competition out there. You can't afford not to get your pictures out to the slicks immediately; if you don't, chances are that someone else will get their pictures out first and make a sale before you even get to market. The market is hungry, and it needs to be fed.

What's in my box? Well, I've got three lenses with me at all times. I have a short, 28-mm lens that I use with a flash when I'm within ten feet of someone. You need the short lens when flashing someone outside a restaurant at night or inside a party, like when I caught Britney smooching Colin Farrell at the Chateau Marmont. I also have a 200-mm lens that I use in low-light situations when I'm at a distance of about fifty feet from the subject. The low-light lens is needed for shooting through tinted windows. More and more pictures are shot through the tint. You can't let them see you.

The classic bazooka lens is the 500-mm, which I have but only use when at distance. I call it the "doubler." It weighs about ten pounds and is very difficult to handle, but when you have to be at distance it's the only way to get the shot. When Tom had me stake out Cameron and Justin in Hawaii, the shot that landed on the cover of *Them!* was of the happy couple kissing on a surf board. I took that shot from almost 200 feet away, and, even with the doubler, it was a little grainy. The world would have never seen that moment were it not for the 500.

But by far the most important lens is my 50-500 mm Sigma zoom lens. That baby cost me $8,000, but it's become standard equipment in this trade. With my Sigma, I can be staked out 150 feet from the subject and snap them tight in total focus, but I also can pull back and get the whole scene in perfect focus. It's a bitchin' lens, dude. It's revolutionized the sport. It allows us to be invisible. And since a lot of the celebs have gotten smart about spotting photogs, it's a necessary weapon in the war.

Of course, I also have a converter that can double my distance. Problem is, lens converters lower the quality, and when you're selling to the slicks the difference between a clean and grainy shot can mean $25,000. The temptation is always there to slap on the converter, but it's lazy to do that. I always say that if you can get a shot at 300 feet, you can get off your ass and get half the distance closer to the subject.

Another important weapon in the arsenal is my Minolta pocket digital. It's only three-quarters of an inch thick, so I can sneak it into any situation. But it also has a nice 39 to 117 mm optical zoom. These cameras are the future. I hear through the grapevine that the CIA is developing a pocket digital with a 28 to 500 mm zoom on it. This baby is the future of the business. We could stand within a hundred feet of a star and conceivably take their picture without them knowing it yet have it look like you were five feet away.

Yeah, it's a pretty expensive business to break into. The lenses and cameras are worth about $30,000, and if you add the cost of my BMW X5 with tinted windows ($52,000), my PowerBook G4 ($2,500) and my wireless Internet account ($1,500 a year), you can see why there are only about fifty professional paparazzi making a good living on the streets of Hollywood. It's just too expensive for most guys to even break in.

Personally, I couldn't have done it had Bronco not helped me out in the beginning. I really owe everything to him. I'm not a cocky guy, but even though he taught me everything he knows, he didn't teach me everything I know.

Like I said, I don't care what equipment I have or don't have. You need a shot, J.B. will get it. J.B. always gets his shot.

TOM PEPPERS

Bureau Chief, Operation Hollywood

Any guy who has nicknamed himself his initials is a weenie. Any guy who then goes and prints his initials on all his clothes and cameras is a super-weenie. Seriously. Go look up "super-weenie" in the dictionary and that's what it says. Or at least it should.

Therefore, Jordie Black is a super-weenie. But I will give credit where it's due: He's the best young paparazzo in the business. He's like a place kicker on a football team: a total mutant but totally necessary.

BARRY POSNER

Special Assistant to the President

When I first met Tom's "team" at the desert base I had my doubts. I mean, who could blame me?

You've got Bronco sitting there with his graying pony tail and wearing a trucker's cap and picking his teeth with a pen cap. You've got surfer-dude Jordie Black in his muscle-T and flip-flops listening to some bad rock music on his iPod. Young and dumb—and cocky.

You've got Jaimee P., cute but so painfully shy she stared at her stubby little feet the entire meeting, unable to make eye contact with anyone, except with Tom. Intense chick.

Then there's Tom, with his expertly coifed hairdo, impeccably facialized skin and wearing a Ryan Seacrest-esque hipster shirt unbuttoned at the top and rolled up at the sleeves. Cheeseball Hollywood guy if there ever was one.

Safe to say, they weren't exactly Delta Force material. But, for better or worse, they were our last best hope of finding Saddam.

WHITE HOUSE PRESS BRIEFING

19 October 2003

Noon

LONDON MARRIOTT: Good afternoon, everyone. I'm going to make a brief statement? And then I'll take some questions? Okay?

(Reading from a TelePrompter.)

The United States of America is winning the war on terror. Thousands of American military men and women have helped restore peace and stability to the Iraqi people. In recent days, our military intelligence officers have brought us one step closer to, as the President likes to say, *smoking out* the country's last vestige of evil, Saddam Hussein. Because the intelligence is classified, we cannot share its details with all of you today, but, rest assured, our great President Bush has complete and total confidence that Saddam Hussein soon will be brought to justice. Thank you.

Now I will take your questions. I'll start with you, the fat, old lady in the front.

HELEN THOMAS, UPI: Ms. Marriott, with all due respect, what the hell are you doing up there?

LONDON: I'm Georgie's—I mean, President Bush's—new secretary.

THOMAS: Secretary of what?

LONDON: The press! Georgie hired me.

THOMAS: Georgie?

LONDON: Yeah. What's the big deal, lady? By the way, can I just say that you really have to stop wearing panty-hose. That's so, like, 1950s.

Okay, next question. John?

JOHN KING, CNN: Ms. Marriott, is the latest intelligence out of Iraq, which you mentioned in your remarks, bringing us any closer to finding Saddam Hussein or his alleged Weapons of Mass Destruction?

LONDON: Weapons of what?

KING: Weapons of *Mass Destruction.* Nuclear, biological, chemical weapons. Have any been found yet?

LONDON: Um ... I don't know. Like, no comment?

KING: Are you asking or telling me "no comment?"

LONDON: Whatever. I mean, who cares? We won the war. Everyone's just got to chill out. Next question, please. Go ahead, Lilly.

LILLY LOHAN, Them! Weekly: London, You look great! Who are you wearing?

LONDON: Thanks so much for asking! Finally, a *real* question. Actually, my dress is Prada and these shoes are Manalo Blahniks. Aren't they cute? My bag is Gucci. I would tell you what's *not* underneath my outfit, but Mr. Rove would get really mad if I told you I wasn't wearing any underwear.

LILLY LOHAN: Well, you do look absolutely *gorgeous*.

LONDON: Thanks so much. So do you!

(Karl Rove jumps to the podium.)

ROVE: That's all the time we have, thank you.

**** TOP SECRET ****

For the President only

20 October 2003

From: Karl Rove, White House Chief Political Strategist

Re: The news weeklies report

Weekly Magazine Newsstand Sales Report

Mag.	**Cover Line**	**Copies Sold**
Them!	"London Takes D.C!"[	[6,859,387]
Us Weekly	"Secrets of London"	[4,555,072]
People	"Hero Pets"	[650,666]
InTouch	"Best Weddings!"	[557,233]
Newsweek	"Still No WMD's!"	[266,129]
Time	"Saddam Still Missing"	[116,665]

GEORGE W. BUSH

President of the United States

I told 'em all to listen to Big George. It was the old bait-and-switch. Look at what happened to those *Them!* sales. London put them out of this world. And *Time* was pretty much ready to fold at that point. No one wanted to read about Saddam. The American public cared more about WD-40 than any WMD. I got the whole country more interested in a hot, little babe than in that mustachioed monster. I thought it was pretty darn brilliant of me, if I don't say as much myself.

I had a master plan—that is, Condi, Mark and I had the plan. But no one else knew what we knew. I couldn't risk the leaks. Had to keep it secret. But the show was working to perfection, just as Mark said it would. We were killing two birds with one stone. We were taking the attention off Saddam's ass and, according to Mark, we were making really good television. Which is always a good thing.

TOM PEPPERS

Bureau Chief, Operation Hollywood

If he weren't so pathetic, it almost would have been a comical presentation. There we sat—the best, highest-paid, most skilled stalkers in the civilian world—and a khaki-clad Barry Posner gets up in front of a chalkboard and starts lecturing us like school children about how the CIA "surveils the enemy."

It got off to a dreadfully condescending start when he walked around the table and he handed us a pamphlet titled "CIA Glossary of Surveillance Terms."

"What the fuck is this shit?" Jordie cracked.

"You've gotta be kidding me," Bronco grumbled. "If you need to read a book on how to follow people, you must not be very good at following people."

Jaimee just glanced at me longingly, as she always does, waiting for me to smile so she could feel good about herself. She's a sweet girl, but she has the self-esteem of a Heidi Fleiss girl. Seriously, I would consider dating Jaimee. Being someone's boss never stopped me before! But I guess I want someone more confident in herself, someone who is not afraid to walk up to me and tell me they want to fuck me. That turns me on. Jaimee's shyness doesn't. Of course, my mother would tell you that my attraction to the girls who come on to me is a function of my fragile ego, that it comes out of a need for me to have female attention in order to stroke my male ego. She might be right. But that's the funny thing about life. Even when you totally know what's wrong, you can't fix the problem. Now that I think of it, isn't that exactly the issue our country has?

Back to Barry's condescending lecture on spying.

"This glossary is so you guys can understand my language," Barry professorially explained. "Take a few minutes to memorize the terms. I'll be back in a half hour." He walked toward the door. He stopped and added with a smirk, "And, yes, there will be a quiz."

As we sat in the spare conference room looking over the terms, I noticed Jordie—the weenie that he is—feverishly scribbling notes all over his pamphlet.

When I asked "J.B." why he was defacing government property, he walked over and dropped his glossary in my lap. At the end of each CIA definition he had cleverly scribbled the equivalent paparazzi term.

Bailout point - The point, during a vehicular run under surveillance, at which the action officer riding as a passenger is planning to bail out of the car in order to elude surveillance. [**Drop out**]

Brief encounter - Any brief physical contact between a case officer and an agent under threat of surveillance. [**Contact**]

Bumper-lock - A harassing move in which vehicular surveillance follows the target officer so closely that the surveilling car's front bumper is almost locked to the rear bumper of the target car. [**Pulling an Arnold**]

Burned - When a case officer or agent is compromised, or a surveillant has been made by a target, usually because they make eye contact. [**Oops-a-doodle]**

Cam-car - A vehicle equipped with a concealed camera used for clandestine casing and surveillance operations. [**Car**]

Casuals - Casual observers to a surveillance exercise; nonparticipants visible in the area. [**Civilians**]

Chokepoint - A narrow passage-such as a bridge, tunnel, or Metro

station-used as a surveillance or countersurveillance tool for channeling the opposing force or monitoring their passage. [**Money spot**]

Cover stop - A stop made while under surveillance that provides an ostensibly innocent reason for a trip. [**Fake out**]

The eye - The person on the surveillance team who has the target under visual observation at any given moment. [**The pap**]

Foots (feet) - Members of a surveillance team who are working on foot and riding as passengers in a surveillance car ("i.e., when the target, a.k.a. rabbit a.k.a. package goes into a building, the team leader

might tell the team to "get two feet in the building" to follow). [**Flashers**]

In the black - Surveillance-free for a time span greater than a few seconds. [**Gone**]

In the wind - When a target of surveillance has escaped and left for parts unknown. [**History**]

Lockstep - When a surveillance team is following so close on foot they seem to be moving in lockstep with the target. [**On 'em**]

OP - An observation post manned by a static surveillant. [**Office**]

Overhead platform - A technical platform, aboard an airplane or satellite, used for technical surveillance and reconnaissance. [**huh?**]

Point - The member of the surveillance team who is following the target from the closest position, the point position. [**Shooter**]

Provocative - A harassing act or procedure designed to flush out

surveillance. [**Snakeout**]

Rabbit - The target in a surveillance operation. [**Famous Fucker**]

Watcher team - A surveillance team usually assigned to a specific target. [**The Boys**]

When Posner returned, I handed him Jordie's artwork.

"What's this?" he asked with his usual confused furrowing of the brow.

"*Our* language," Jordie snapped back. "You're the one who's going to have to learn to speak to *us*. We're the professionals here."

As much as I hated to admit it, I agreed with the weenie.

"He's right, Barry," I said. "We know how to follow people who don't want to be followed. How do you think Bronco got Ben Affleck doing that hooker in the alley? How do you think Jaimee got Reese Witherspoon yelling at her dopey husband? How do you think Jordie got the first shot of Madonna's baby? We're pros. We appreciate your efforts, but the last I checked we don't have time for nursery school. We're the ones who will rake in six million dollars if we find the bastard. We'd listen to you if we thought it would help, but I'm sorry to report that it ain't one bit."

To his credit, Posner took it like a man. It was sad, actually. Here's a guy who had dedicated his entire professional career to the tradecraft of a CIA officer, yet would have trouble finding a fat guy in a Taco Bell.

"Fine," Barry said, near tears. "You guys can go about it however you want."

"Damn right, we will!" Jordie piped in from the end of the table.

"Look, Barry," I said. "Just tell us where to start and we'll go find him. Simple as that."

"But it's not that simple," he replied. "This isn't going to be like finding Michael Jackson on vacation in Maui. This isn't like snapping a photo of Tom Cruise playing grab-ass. This is going to be the toughest assignment of your lives. You'll be shot at, laughed at, shouted at in a language you don't even understand, you'll stick out like whores in a church. And, oh, I haven't told you yet: You can't use your own equipment."

BARRY POSNER

Special Assistant to the President

You should have seen the looks on their faces when I told them they couldn't bring their toy boxes to Iraq. I mean, even Bronco's dark skin turned the color of Crest. Priceless, is what it was. But at least I got their attention.

Finally, they were shocked to silence long enough for me to outline their mission to them. Using the TinyShot™ digital cameras developed by the CIA (though about the size of a Kit Kat, they are more powerful and shoot sharper images than a standard 500-mm paparazzi camera), they were to conduct surveillance on and photograph every Iraqi taxi driver and passenger engaged in suspicious activity. And the key was to do it without the subjects knowing they're being photographed. Like they said, this is what the paparazzi claimed to be experts at. If they got lucky, they might even track down Saddam.

Another thing that blew them away was that the TinyShot™ functioned as video and still cameras with equal effectiveness. That meant that everything they shot would be transmitted back to Washington in video form as well. But most important were the still pictures. The only real way to identify these Saddam loyalists was from still images, which these misfits were most skilled at capturing.

So why did we need pictures so badly? And why did we have to recruit these celebrity stalkers to take them? Not to get too technical on you, but over the last few years CIA agents had been photographing the faces of every member of Saddam's inner circle—from his cook, to his personal driver, to every member of his cabinet. You name a close adviser, and we've got their image stored back in our FacePrint™ system. So if we got a positive ID on a taxi driver being a member of Saddam's inner circle, we could then put that taxi on round-the-clock satellite and drone surveillance, in the hope that they would lead us to the Butcher of Baghdad.

SADDAM HUSSEIN

Former President of Iraq

Oh, those stupid American politicians! Those infidels, those sons of Satan! Mr. Bush and his cowardly soldiers were trying so hard to find me. They had all their Western gadgets, their high-tech instruments of evil probing the world in search of the Great One. If they only had known how easy it would have been to find me. Hahahaha! George Bush and his feeble brain!

They used their television and newspapers to make propaganda against me and the people of Iraq. Even your venerable *New York Times* believed their lies that I was harboring weapons. They tried to make Saddam look like the evil one. But they forgot that I am the Glorious Leader, the true Lion of Babylon.

Most important, the foolish criminals simply forgot how much I loved to swim at the beach. Silly Americans. Splat. I spit on them! When you act justly you have the gods as allies. I always tell the truth. Just because the Americans needed a reason to, as they say, "finish the job" Mr. Bush's father failed to complete, they made up lies. Saddam believes that false words are not only evil in themselves, but they infect the soul with evil. Mr. Bush has infected his country's soul.

I must admit that America does have the most beautiful women and the finest burritos. Venice Beach sure beats the coast of Basra!

BARRY POSNER

Special Assistant to the President

Unlike the pre-war days, when our agents were snapping TinyShot™ images of unsuspecting Saddam loyalists, the environment had turned hostile and Saddam's loyalists became very aware of being followed and watched.

The Predator drone aircraft was equipped with a very powerful camera lens and we could get fairly vivid images of movement on the ground in Iraq. However, the Predator had to fly at an altitude of less than two-thousand feet to capture a facial image that would *maybe* be clear enough for our FacePrint™ software to store the data.

Therefore, in order to capture useable images, the subject's face needed to be turned at least thirty-five degrees toward the camera and, even with the TinyShot™ digital cameras, the subject could be no further than fifty yards away. It was clear to everyone at the CIA not only that we needed to get feet on the ground, but that we needed skilled photographers. Hence President Bush's idea to recruit these vapid celebrity chasers. Not a bad idea, in theory.

So it seemed like a fairly plausible plan. We'd give the paparazzi tiny-but-powerful cameras, put Peppers in charge of managing these unique personalities, then ship them off to Iraq, where they'd shoot hundreds of facial images of men we suspected were in Saddam's inner-circle. The images would instantly be transmitted back to Langley, where a FacePrint™ would be created on the computer. The techies at Langley were excited about this new biometrics technology, which uses biological information to verify identity.

Not to get too nerdy on you, but every face has certain distinguishing characteristics, varying peaks and valleys that comprise facial features. In techspeak, we call them "nodal points." Anyway, the computer scans the photo and these nodal points are measured and identified by a string of numbers. It measures the things like the distance between eyes, width of a nose, depth of eye sockets, protrusion of cheekbones, jaw line and the shape of a chin. This series of numbers makes up a FacePrint™. It's like a fingerprint, but for the face. But in order for the computer to recognize a face, the image has to be clear enough and taken at good enough angle to identify approximately twenty nodal points. Essentially, our plan was to locate, identify and then follow with GPS tracking those hundred or so Saddam loyalists whom we suspected knew Saddam's whereabouts.

At the time, this FacePrint™ technology and the TinyShot™ cameras were the latest and greatest gadgets in our spook arsenal, and the CIA couldn't wait to employ them in the field.
In retrospect, the paparazzi might have been the right choice, but I regret not giving them more training. If I had not caved to Dr. Rice's pressure to get boots on the ground in Baghad, a lot of pain and hurt would have been avoided.

**** TOP SECRET ****

For the President only

02 November 2003

From: Karl Rove, White House Chief Political Strategist

Re: The news weeklies report

Weekly Magazine Newsstand Sales Report

Mag.	**Cover Line**	**Copies Sold**
Them!	"London&George's Love"	[9,759,881]
Us	"Bush Takes London!"	[6,873,923]
People	"50 Most Anorexic Stars"	[1,690,866]
InTouch	"Kelly Ripa Cheats!"	[983,246]
Time	"Where the Hell is Saddam??"	[17,486]
Newsweek	"Still No WMD's!"	[9,034]

THE OVAL OFFICE

03 November 2003

11:13 a.m.

BUSH: London, I gotta hand it to you, gal. You're doin' a real bang-up job handling the media. The magazines are eatin' it up. Real bang-up. No pun intended, of course.

LONDON: No pun taken, sir. And, by the way, I have to thank you for everything, Mr. President.

BUSH: Call me George.

LONDON: How about Georgie?

BUSH: That's fine, honey. Heck, a young girl as cute as you can call me whatever you like. ... And speakin' of young, how old do you think I look?

LONDON: Oh, Georgie, I don't know. Let me see here ...

(London, in a black micro-mini skirt and tight-fitting pink sweater, walks sexily around Bush, scanning him from head to toe.)

LONDON: I'd guess, like, 42-ish?

BUSH: Really? You think so? Even with these gray hairs that have sprouted up in the last year?

LONDON: You look *really* good for your age, *Mister President.* Trust me.

BUSH: Well, I'm 55. But I bet you still think Bill Clinton looks better, don't ya? I mean, the guy's grayer than me, you know.

LONDON: Let's not talk about him, sir. I was in high school when he was president. I'm most interested in you. You are my boss, after all.

SECRETARY [on intercom]: Mr. President, your wife is here to see you.

BUSH: Uh ... well ... uh ... tell her to, uh, hold on a sec. Better yet, tell her I'm in a very important meetin', would ya?

LONDON: Oh, Georgie, but I'd love to meet the First Lady! Pretty please? I've never met a First Lady before. I mean, like I've met

Oprah and stuff, but never a First Lady. I promise I'll be good.

BUSH: Look, London, I've been under a lot of pressure lately, and, you know, being the President and all, it's important that I maintain a –

LONDON: Don't speak. You don't have to say anything. I'm a big girl. I know what's *really* on your mind.

BUSH: What's that?

LONDON: The war, of course. Duh!

BUSH: Yes, it is. The war. You betcha.

(London raises a skeptical eyebrow)

BUSH: Okay, maybe a lot.

LONDON: My mother told me you're the most powerful man in the free world. And, well, I just think that's so ... so sexy. We should have a drink some time after work.

(London walks to Bush and stands three inches in front of him and starts adjusting his tie.)

BUSH: I thank you for your support, and your *optimism* is very much appreciated. But, Ms. Marriott, I quit drinkin' over ten years ago, haven't had a lick since I re-dedicated my life to Jesus.

LONDON: I love Jesus too! I have a really cool "Jesus is My Homeboy" t-shirt. But I understand. If there's ever anything I can do to help you with your stress, you just call me. Here (she hands him her cell phone number). Now, I don't give this out to many people, but, for you, I'd do anything.

BUSH: I appreciate that and, in fact, I'll take you up on that offer right now. So could you slide on out the back door here before Laura sees you with me in here alone?

(London struts out of the Oval Office and into the Rose Garden, blowing the rosy-cheek President a kiss.)

LONDON: *Ciao,* baby.

GEORGE W. BUSH

President of the United States

I know some people think of me as a fool. But there's a method to my madness. In the case of hunting down Saddam, I had a theory goin'. I called it the Theory of Twos.

The theory is based on this idea: I believe in all my heart that the American people can only focus on two main famous personalities in the popular culture at a time. In other words, when you think of *Baywatch*, who comes to mind? I bet it's Pam Anderson and David Hasselhoff. *Two people*. You followin' me? I'm tellin' ya, it's a fool-proof theory! Here's another one for ya: We don't think of Britney Spears being in competition with a slew of other hot, young things; we only think of Britney versus Christina Aguilera.

The same went for this whole war thing. The American people were fixated on two things: me and Saddam. This posed a serious problem, seeing as though we had neither killed nor captured the hairy bugger. So I had to get the people focused on a different person, someone as *opposite* of Saddam as you could get. And, my friend, who is more polar opposite of Saddam Hussein than London Marriott? Exactly. Nobody is.

Mark—he's a real genius—had me convinced that those celebrity magazine sales were the best barometer of what people cared about, and, judging by the sales of *Time* and *Newsweek*, obviously no one cared about WMD's or the fact that Saddam was still MIA. Those drab newsmagazine sales were dropping faster than my daddy's approval ratings back in 1992.

Thank God that Arnold put me in touch with Mark. Had he not, I might still be sitting here wondering how in the hell we are going to spin the fact that Saddam Hussein had been living in Venice Beach while we spent billions of dollars looking for him in Iraq.

I knew I couldn't play that George-and-London game for long. Too smart for that. First of all, Laura was gettin' pretty peeved at me spendin' so much time with the gal, what with all the magazine rumors about extra-marital hanky panky and so forth. Ari Fleischer, London is not—if you know what I mean. She certainly has nicer hair! Heheheh. Aw, heck.

Anyways. Second of all, I knew that pretty soon the American people, being the smartest people in the world, would eventually remember that Saddam remained free and we had to catch him. That's why I told Barry and Condi to wrap things up by the first of the year.

I wasn't lying. I gave them a job to do and a deadline to do it by. So, okay, maybe they didn't know the big picture of what else was going on. But you gotta compartmentalize information when it comes to undercover operations. Can't let everyone know everything all the time. As Daddy always said, "Not gonna do that at this juncture." I didn't want to risk a leak when I only told Rummy I was plannin' Operation Iraqi Freedom, and I didn't want to do it for Operation Hollywood.

MARK BURTON

Executive Producer, *Who Wants To Be An American Hero*

I don't like the term "reality television." People have come to use it in a demeaning way, as if there's television, and then there's a lesser-form of entertainment that I produce. Technically, the shows I make are not at all reality, but, rather, a carefully crafted version of it meant to manipulate the audience's thoughts and feelings in a certain way. That's why I prefer to call it "unscripted" television.

You simply create a situation and watch people react to it. What we're creating is not real; yes, it's a part of the reality, but it's only the stuff we've chosen to show you. Reality is the combination of that edited stuff you see, plus everything we do not show viewers.

I've learned that America wants a good story that they can relate to, a story filled with characters that remind them of themselves and the people they know. This isn't a want; it's a *need.* They don't care if it is true. They just want it to reinforce what they already believe: That there's a God, that America is a just nation and that TV is a good thing. Look, if the Bible were a TV reality show, it would be the first reality program and Jesus the first reality star. Now that would have been one hell of a reality program! I would have called it, "Who Wants to Believe in Jesus?" I'd sell it to CBS and they'd run it on Sunday nights, after *Survivor.* The heartland would love it.

I suppose it was inevitable that I'd end up producing a political show. Politicians have been employing the tools of reality TV for years. They run commercials aimed to manipulate you into voting for them. They stage photo-ops to project a desired image. They give speeches to persuade you to believe their version of the truth, not to inform you of the facts. The State of the Union address is the consummate reality show!

I'd argue that producers like me, who edit shows into a distorted version of reality, are merely copying our political colleagues. So when Arnold told me that President Bush might be able to use my talents in the White House, I just had to be a part of it. It was the next step for me, the ultimate use of my skills to tell a compelling, dramatic story using real-life characters and real-life situations.

The president was supportive from our very first meeting in his office. It was mid-September, a few months into the war in Iraq, and the poor guy looked exhausted, like he hadn't slept in weeks. The bags under his eyes were so big I'd call them luggage.

"Mark," he said weakly, "Ever since we invaded Iraq, I've been so focused on winning over Iraqis that I forgot that we need to win over the hearts and minds of the American people."

"Yes, sir," I said. "That's the goal of every show I produce, to win over America. And our scorecard is the Nielsen ratings."

"I know," he replied, "that's why you are here. Arnold said you were just the man who could help."

Like I said, Bush looked just awful. Pathetic. On TV, he'd always looked hawkish to me. But sitting just six feet in front of him, I thought he looked owlish. Gone was that glint in his eye, that cowboy swagger in his step. He looked like a defeated man. I didn't understand why he seemed so forlorn. "With all due respect, why are you so down on your war effort?" I asked. "From what I can tell, you have nearly all of Iraq under control, you are beginning to hand over some governmental authority to the Iraqi people, and you are getting closer every day to finding Saddam."

"Actually, Mark, we have found Saddam."

"That's great!"

Bush's ashen, expressionless face told me that not only was I naïve, but I was wrong.

"No," he replied, handing me torn-out page out of a glossy magazine. "It's not great. In fact, it's a problem. And you gotta help me solve it, buddy."

I looked at the paper to find it was a page out of *Them!* magazine, one of the seemingly dozens of celebrity-driven rags that fill the newsstands. At the top of the page in big red letters it read "CELEBRITY LOOK-ALIKE OF THE WEEK!" And below that was a photo of a bushy-haired man who looked like Saddam Hussein. He had a long beard and was wearing shorts, a Mickey Mouse t-shirt and a pair of thong sandals. The photo caption read, "You saw it here first! A *Them!* photographer found this man resembling a certain former Middle East dictator collecting cans on the boardwalk at Venice Beach. When asked why he was at a sunny L.A. beach and not the Middle East, the man replied in a thick Arabic accent, 'The sands here remind me of the desert sands of Iraq.' Only in L.A., dear readers. Only in L.A. ... "

I looked up at Bush, who had stood up and begun staring out the window looking out at the South Lawn. Still gazing out the window, Bush said to me, "So what do you think?"

"You're right," I told him. "You really do need my help.

JESSICA PEPPERS

Tom Peppers's Hot Wife

I honestly believe that throughout our two years of marriage that Tom never cheated on me—that is, except for the time with London. To be honest with you, I wasn't as mad about him poking that little skank as I was about everyone in the world knowing about it. Filing for divorce was the only way to, you know, maintain my dignity.

It was doomed anyway. Our marriage had become a dull, boring exercise in domestication. Tom was married to his work, not me. I had grown married to avoiding work at all costs. I enjoyed the freedom of going to the gym every morning, taking daily jogs with celebrity trainer Gunnar Peterson, hitting the nail salon two times a week, taking a weekly Power Yoga class with celebrity yogi Brian Kest. I mean, my only obligation to Tom was to have sex with him, which wasn't that bad most of the time.

He made a lot of money, and he could get us reservations at any L.A. restaurant, but our relationship lacked any real passion. I started to think that maybe I had made a mistake, that maybe I should have pulled a Jennifer Aniston and picked the hot guy over the all-around-package guy. So, yeah, after that whole London Marriott mess went down the thought of going back to Jordie did cross my mind. But I can never go back. Never. I am not the type to break up and get back together. I end it and move on. Life's too short to waste time trying to fix relationships that are doomed from the start. I know guys have trouble understanding this, but it's just the way it has to be. Once a woman's made up her mind, it's almost impossible to change it; whereas a guy can change his mind about a girl the second she decides she wants to bang him.

I'm a Scorpio. Normally, I don't like to bring up astrological stuff because, whenever I do, people just assume I am another zodiac-babbling L.A. blonde. But I'm serious about it. Being a Scorpio is all you need to know about me. Scorpios are determined and forceful, emotional and intuitive, powerful and passionate, exciting and magnetic. (On the darker side, we're also jealous, resentful, secretive, obsessive and obstinate.) But what really freaks guys out—especially Aries and Leos—is that Scorpio is the symbol of sex. We are the most sensual of all the astrological signs.

One of my astrological books even describes the typical Scorpio as "capable of great heights of passionate transport, but debauchery and perversion are always dangers, and Scorpios can become sadistic monsters of sensuality and eroticism."

So, like, I know I am scary to guys. Tom is an Aries, which is not good for him, poor guy. Arians are so innocent that they are drawn to the danger of Scorpios like me because they are so trusting. Being an Aries, Tom tends to be adventurous, impulsive, enthusiastic and so optimistic that it often blinds him from reality. I think Tom ended up cheating on me because, deep down, he knew I was out of his league, that I would end up leaving him eventually anyway. Which is true. Or at least that's what my reader told me the other day.

As if I even need to tell you, Jordie is a classic Cancer. On the plus side, he is emotional and loving, intuitive and imaginative, shrewd and cautious. On the minus side, he's an overemotional and clingy mess of a moody man. Cancers are so pathetic, though I'm much more suited to be with a Cancer than an Aries because, well, Cancers tend to worship me while Aries tend to try to control me. Men are the inferior gender. So it's sad that almost all the people in charge of the world are men.

My favorite band in the world, Counting Crows, has, like, my favorite song. It's called Yellow Taxi, a remake of some old chick's song. Anyway, in the song the lead singer Adam Duritz sings, "Sometimes you don't know what you got till it's gone. You paved paradise and put up a parking lot." Well, the more I thought about things the more I felt like Tom was a fucking parking lot.

JORDIE BLACK

Photographer, Operation Hollywood

When Burton tracked me down at my Venice apartment that daylast summer, I was ready for a change. Luckily, he needed memore than I needed him. It was a recipe for me to get what I really wanted: Jessica.

"I'm here to talk to you about that guy you photographed for *Them!*," Burton told me, his British accent of his rolling off his tongue like a wet tea bag.

"What picture?" I asked.

"The one of the guy who looks like Saddam Hussein." "Oh," I said. "That homeless dude?" I didn't realize why he would want to talk to that guy. I added, "What, you are doing a dating show for the homeless?"

"Something like that," he said, all serious and stuff.

"I just need to find him for something."

I wasn't about to let the guy off the hook that easily. I could tell by the crinkles around his eyes that he really needed to find that homeless loser I had found schlepping in the sand at Venice.

"Why do you need him so badly?" I asked.

"Honestly," Burton said, "it's for TV show."

"What kind of show?"

"A reality show."

"Can I be in it?"

Soon after I became a photographer, I realized that the easiest way to become rich wasn't stalking the famous but to become famous myself. And, nowadays, there's no faster way to become famous than to get your ass on a reality show, so that's honestly why I wanted to be on a reality show. It had become obvious to me that a reality show would be my ticket to the kind of fame that would let me never have to work again. And maybe, I though, I could woo Jessica back.

"Sure, you can be in it," Mark said. "But if you don't tell me where I can find that homeless Hussein, then we have no reality show."

"So, let's say I bring him to you," I said. "What's in it for me?"

"What do you want?"

"To be in the show," I said, pausing, then adding, "and I want something else."

"You name it," he said. And I could tell he meant it.

"I want you to break up a marriage for me," I said.

Two weeks later, the London tape with Tom Peppers was leaked to the media and—predictably—Tom came knocking for me and Bronco. The plan was working to perfection.

BRONCO

Photographer, Operation Hollywood

Most technology makes all of us expendable and, eventually, obsolete. From the moment Barry handed me that TinyShot™ camera during our meeting in the desert I realized I might as well have been clutching my executioner's gun.

I should have seen it coming. First, the cameras got easier to use. No longer did you have to be a trained photographer to take paparazzi shots. Rather, you could train yourself how to adjust for light and distance conditions in just a matter of days. Then came the digitals, eliminating the need for lab technicians, eliminating any need for any of the darkroom skills I had acquired back in college. Then the cameras got smaller and more lightweight, opening the door for skinny guys and young women to become paparazzi. And now comes the TinyShot™, a technology

I feared when it came on to the market in the next year or so would turn the art of paparazzi-style photography into little more than a point-and-shoot outing at Disneyland, an endeavor accessible to anyone who could afford the camera and had the ability to spot and track celebrities. The game was changing.

As our plane descended over the barren desert of western Iraq headed for touchdown at Baghdad Airport, I felt overcome with a foreboding sense that on this trip I'd be playing the endgame. I realized that we'd better find Saddam and collect the dough because, when we got back home, it only would be a matter of months before the party would be over. Old-school paps like me, with our old-school cameras and old-school toy boxes, soon would be like Bob Hope and Marlon Brando—fossils of a bygone Hollywood era.

I saw the writing on the wall. We'd soon become as out-dated as the workers on the car-assembly line who were replaced by robotic arms, or the toll attendants replaced by optical scanning machines, or the classically trained actors who found Hollywood fame and fortune until they were replaced by average Joes and Jills who go on reality dating shows to get famous and get laid.

When the plane touched down in Baghdad, I looked out the window and saw the airfield's stark, arid landscape, thinking that my career back home would soon be as bleak.

Suddenly, I had a motivation for finding Saddam beyond mere patriotic duty; I needed that six-million dollars. I was forty-six. I didn't have enough money for retirement. I had made a lot of money, but I'd also spent a lot. The advent of the TinyShot™ era would mark the end of my prime earning years, and, as such, I was faced with a choice: Find Saddam, or risk being as irrelevant as *Time* and *Newsweek*.

The challenge would be the greatest of my career. The sprawl of Baghdad, the mass of mud huts and tan apartment shanties, looked imposing and impenetrable. We weren't in Malibu. We were heading into a city where none of us had ever been, on an assignment that would be harder than any of us could have ever imagined. But we had our cameras, and we had each other. Thank God, we had Tom Peppers leading us.

JAIMEE P.

Photographer, Operation Hollywood

As Tom has told us a million times in staff meetings, morale is the single greatest factor in winning a war. Luckily, besides Jordie, whose the level of happiness is only as high as the money he's making at the time, everyone on the team had very high morale heading into Iraq. I loved those guys like brothers. That is, except for Tom. I loved him in a different way. Not that he had any damn idea.

Tom was a born leader. From the moment we hopped in the Humvee and rolled through the ambush alleys of downtown Baghdad, watching a dizzying blur of taxicabs carrying god-knows-who, Tom had us all convinced that despite the overwhelming odds our photographs would help find Saddam Hussein. He has the ability to make you believe in yourself. The tiny cameras made it even easier. On our first day, I must have snapped a couple dozen taxi drivers and sent them back to Washington for analysis. It felt so good to be doing a job that was for the greater good. But everywhere we looked there was reason to doubt we could pull it off. And Jordie's negative attitude didn't help at all.

"How the fuck are we going to shoot every taxi in this town?" a typically pessimistic Jordie snapped. "We'll be here for the next ten years shooting cars. They'll kill us before then!"

Tom, however, remained calm, reading the CIA briefing books on Saddam's loyalists and books on Iraqi tribal culture. If he shared the same doubts he never let on. In the field, Tom is like a computer, constantly downloading the data around him until he has enough information to formulate a plan of attack. It doesn't matter if it's a fallen dictator or a hot-shot celebrity. He always does his homework.

On a personal level, I wanted to cry when the women on the street in front of the hotel started throwing rocks at my legs and shouting in Arabic, "Infidel! Infidel!" ... I asked Barry why they were throwing rocks at me and he said it was because I was wearing shorts. Apparently, in Muslim society women have to cover their bodies from head to ankle, so I changed immediately into a long skirt borrowed from a Swedish journalist staying at the hotel.

Despite the oppressive heat, the sexist society, the immense danger, I was excited to be in Iraq. For the first in my photography career I'd be shooting subjects who weren't celebrities.

Bronco, however, was subdued. On our first day, Barry thought it would help us to do a ride-along with an Army platoon through the city. Maybe the heat—it was about a hundred degrees—was getting to him, or maybe he was having trouble recovering from the twenty-hour flight. Maybe he felt lost without his old Canons slung over his shoulder. Whatever the reason, Bronco wasn't his normal cheerful, alert self. I can't help but think if the real Bronco had been in that Humvee with us, that the tragedy might not have happened.

**** TOP SECRET****

For the President only

14 November 2003

To: George Bush, The President of the United States

From: Karl Rove, White House Chief Political Strategist

Re: The "news" weeklies report

Weekly Magazine Newsstand Sales Report

Mag.	**Cover Line**	**Copies Sold**
Them!	"London for Veep!"	[2,478,003]
Newsweek	"Where is Saddam?"	[1,369,809]
Us	"London's Secrets"	[956,002]
People	"Reality TV Mania"	[924,395]
InTouch	"Reality Botox Babes"	[779,378]
Time	"Inside Alzheimer's"	[17,361]

THE RUSH LIMBAUGH RADIO SHOW

15 November 2003

12:22 p.m.

LIMBAUGH: Ladies and gentlemen, we have a very, very, very special guest with us on this fine program today. We are joined by the beautiful, young and talented new White House press secretary, London Marriott. London, welcome to the Excellence in Broadcasting network.

LONDON: It's so excellent to be here, Rush.

LIMBAUGH: Okay, Ms. Marriott, let's cut right to the chase. The East Coast liberal media elite would have us all believe that you were hired by the Bush administration a few months ago in order to distract the American public from the alleged failures of our war effort in Iraq. Would you like to tell our listeners just how absurd that notion is?

LONDON: It's sooo absurd, Rush. Totally absurd.

LIMBAUGH: I thought so. And might I add that you are doing a tremendous job fending off those liberal elitists in the White House press corps. Your wit and beauty just disarms them, and it's something great to watch.

Now, let's take a call. Brian from the great state of Florida, you are on with London Marriott.

BRIAN: Mega dittoes, Rush!

LIMBAUGH: Extra-mega dittoes back at you. What's your question, Brian?

BRIAN: My question is actually for you, Rush. Do you know where I can score a few thousand Oxycontin, because I really could use a dose of –

LIMBAUGH: Whoa! Now that was just uncalled for. No doubt that guy was an operative for the Democratic camp! Mr. Snerdley, my producer, you must do a better job of screening these calls. Too many liberal crazies out there! Let's try this again. Donna, from Raleigh, North Carolina. You are on with the most beautiful woman in politics and, if I may add, the most handsome man you'll find across the fruited plain.

DONNA: Big Southern Dittos out to you, Rush. And, London, I was just want to say that y'all doing a fine job and we support you. A lot of folks have a trouble accepting a strong, smart, attractive woman. And I applaud y'all for doing such a great job for our country.

LONDON: You're so sweet. I really appreciate that. Americans rock!

DONNA: All my pleasure, London. But I was fixin' to ask you a question. Do y'all think our fightin' men and women over in Iraq are close to finding that pesky Saddam?

LIMBAUGH: Excellent question, Donna. The liberals would have you believe that all Americans are stupid and don't have a mind for themselves. But I've always said that the EIB has the smartest listeners in all of the fruited plain. What's the answer, Ms. Marriott?

LONDON: I'm so glad you asked that, Donna, because, in fact, we are very close. Any day now, actually. Like, I am told they're getting real close.

LIMBAUGH: You heard it here first, folks. Despite what the liberal media would have you believe, Saddam Hussein is in our cross hairs. I understand you have a very important briefing to attend back in Washington. Thanks for taking the time to speak to us, Ms. Marriott.

LONDON: It was all my pleasure, Rush. I have to say before I go that I've had sort of a crush on you—that is, after you lost the weight and stuff.

LIMBAUGH: Well, I love your work too, Ms. Marriott.

LONDON: Rushford, I have a feeling we could bond over pharmaceuticals and stuff.

LIMBAUGH: Uh, well, you know ... um. We've run out of time, Dittoheads! But we'll be back after these messages. You're listening to the EIB radio network.

LONDON MARRIOTT

White House Press Secretary

Rush wasn't nearly as fat as I thought he would be. Like, I thought he would be Santa Claus fat, but he was more like Norm-from-*Cheers* fat.

Meeting people like Rush and getting such awesome experience being on camera and on radio shows was really the best training I could ever get for being a media personality. And Mark Burton is a total TV genius. Like he has the best ideas about how to make people pay attention to you. He's got a sixth, seventh and even eighth sense for these things. Do you really think that my first sex tape—the one of me having sex with my boyfriend Rick—was made public by total accident? You kidding! That was Mark's idea. A lot of people don't realize that Mark does a lot of consulting for celebrities and politicians who pay him *a lot* of money to refashion their reality image. Mark's favorite thing to say is "perception is reality." The guy is saying it, like, all the time. I guess he's helped a lot of people, way before Georgie hired him. Mark oversaw the transformation of Arnold's image from an ass-spanking womanizer to a respectable governor. And, well, everyone knows what he did for Ronald Stump. That's no secret. With *The Assistant*, Mark turned a pompous dude with a totally rancid hairdo into a likeable guy.

What did I learn from my experience? Well, it would have to be that being a secretary is really hard work. It's more than just standing at the podium and reading statements and looking hot in tight skirts. Okay, that's most of the job, but definitely not everything.

GEORGE W. BUSH

President of the United States

It was Mark's idea to start monitoring those weekly magazine sales. And thank God we did. Sales of that *Newsweek* cover asking where Saddam were troubled me. That boring magazine was the number-two bestseller of the week! Granted, the London Marriott cover on *Them!* was still the top-seller, but I knew instinctively that it was time to get that damn Saddam because I sensed that I was losing the audience.

You gotta remember your audience. Ronald Reagan was the master of playing to the audience. I learned a thing or two from him on that score. Now, it might come as a surprise to you that I am not a very analytical guy, don't spent a lot of time thinking about myself, about why I do things. Go with my gut. Go with my *instincts*. My instinct told me that I was doing the right thing. I didn't stop and worry about what Dick or Rummy thought. I was running out of time to win the hearts and minds of the American people on this Iraq thing.

It was December, and the re-election was only eleven long months away. It woulda been nice to wait to get him until a little closer to the election, but what the hell ya gonna do? I asked Mark to wrap things up right quick. We had to act decisively and quickly. That's what presidents do.

TOM PEPPERS

Bureau Chief, Operation Hollywood

The "cover" in Iraq that the CIA gave us was that we were Canadian journalists on special assignment from *Northern Exposure* magazine. Barry had supplied us with phony passports and media credentials, and the CIA guys had stitched maple leafs on all of our baggage and even placed little maple leaf stickers on our TinyShot™, or, as Bronco had fancied them, "our Weapons of Mass Documentation." I have to hand it to those guys at the CIA. They might not have had any clue how to find Saddam, but they were otherwise real good at this James Bond stuff. They can create foreign birth certificates, driver's licenses, phony credit cards with phony credit histories. They even aged the documents so they didn't look like they were a few weeks old, which they were. Impressive stuff.

But our government's understanding of what's happening in Iraq is not nearly as impressive. It doesn't take an Islamic scholar to figure out that Iraqis generally hate Americans. Oddly enough, though, they don't mind Canadians. During his reign Saddam had brainwashed the populace into thinking that Canada was their friend because its government let thousands of Iraqis attend all their universities, ignoring the fact that Canada always had lent military support to virtually every Allied war campaign. Should anyone have asked, Barry—who still was toting around that annoying hand-held video camera everywhere we went—told us we were to say we were working on a feature story about taxicab culture in Iraq. It seemed ridiculous enough to be believable.

But on our first day Barry had the bright idea that all of us should get oriented to the confusing Baghdad street geography by going on a ride-along with a platoon in the Adhamiya District, a densely populated neighborhood along the Tigris River in the northern part of the city. Adhamiya is one of Baghdad's oldest, and also the most Saddam-friendly area of the city. The Army platoon leader warned us that on a daily basis they were the target of RPG's (Rocket Propelled Grenades), IED's (Improvised Explosive Devices), grenades and gunfire. Willie, the redneck platoon leader, told us in a gentle drawl, "Put on your helmet, flak jacket and kevlar body armor. Y'all just might need it."

Bronco, Jaimee, Jordie and I hopped into the back of a roofless high-back Humvee and just like that we began our journey to find Saddam. Barry sat up front with Willie.

"I'd be one broke pap if I drove this battle ax in L.A.," Jordie whined as our convoy barreled down a one-way street, drawing the attention of anyone within a mile. "It would be like, 'Hey, Madonna, look! It's me, over here in the back of this armored truck, next to the guys with M-16's. I'm snapping photos of you. But, really, Madonna, act normal for the camera!'" It was a rare moment of hilarity from an otherwise unfunny egomaniac.

What happened next was not at all funny.

We rolled slowly down Imam Street, the main thoroughfare, past a busy marketplace and bustling sidewalks lined with teahouses and restaurants. It was a Tuesday afternoon, yet it looked like a holiday, as if no one had a job, which in fact had been the case ever since the invasion. Drab yellow and orange taxicabs filled the streets, causing me to think that the intelligence about Saddam getting around in taxis was not so much intelligent information as *obvious* information.

One of our armed escort-soldiers pointed across the street to the Abu Hanifa mosque, where Saddam was last seen in public until his seven-month disappearance into the Iraqi underground. You might recall the TV images of Saddam surrounded by chanting loyalists, clouds of smoke from U.S. bombing wafting in the distance. The uniformed dictator even kissed a baby. A real charmer, that Saddam. "If Saddam's still in Baghdad," Barry shouted to us over the roar of the tank leading our convoy, "chances are he's somewhere in this neighborhood."

I was both excited to be at Ground Zero and terrified by the landscape. It was as if we were on the Universal Studios back lot, touring the set of a third-world Middle Eastern city populated by menacing-looking actors dressed like Arabs. But this wasn't Hollywood. Down the alleys weren't gift shops, but rather angry Iraqis ready to take us out just for looking American.

I glanced at the top of the mosque's clock tower, which was damaged by tank shells a few months ago in a week-long battle for control of this neighborhood. That had to have pissed them off. From what I've read about Muslim society, blowing up one of their mosques is like one of them blowing up Yankee Stadium.

As I studied the pock marks and pondered how pissed off these people must be at Americans, I heard a loud clunk. It sounded like a large rock had landed in our flatbed. I looked down and saw a Pepsi can wrapped in tape rolling on the bed. Then, as if in slow motion, the can rolled to a stop at Bronco's feet. Bronco smiled. As he picked up the can with both hands, Barry shouted, "Bomb!"

In that split second, Bronco realized that the soda can was in fact one of the Improvised Explosive Devices that the platoon leader had warned us about, a can filled with nuts and bolts and glass shards and gun powder. A wick was sticking straw-like out of the top. Some Iraqi had just served us a lethal cocktail.

Everyone in the truck bed immediately curled up in a ball and ducked for cover. I jumped on top of Jaimee to protect her. Jordie shoved his head between his legs, airplane-crash style. Barry, sitting in the front cab, must have simply crouched down. As Bronco's smile instantly was replaced with utter terror he went to toss the device overboard. But it was too late.

The can exploded in an ear-popping flash, propelling a shower of metal and glass into the surrounding area. Shrapnel ricocheted off the truck walls and onto our helmets, arms and legs. Luckily, all of us had on body armor. A medic later told us that if it had been an actual grenade, we'd all have suffered serious injuries, lost limbs, not to mention copious amounts of blood. But since the IED had the force of a few M-80s, the only team member to suffer those injuries, sadly enough, was Bronco.

I looked up and saw blood pouring out of both his arms as he raised his arms up to see that the makeshift grenade had blown his hands to shreds.

MARK BURTON

Executive Producer, *Who Wants To Be An American Hero*

Any reality TV show worth the video on which it's shot features seven key elements.

1) **The Hero (-es).** For example, in *The Assistant*, that man was Ronald Stump. *The Eatery* had the hot, young New York chef. In the case of *Who Wants To Be An American Hero*, it was President Bush—our fearless, cowboy-like, no-nonsense leader, along with his scrappy band of truth-seeking paparazzi.

2) **The Anti-hero**. Obviously, Saddam Hussein fit this role perfectly. What person could be more un-American than Saddam? He was the perfect villian, brilliant reality casting, if I don't say so myself.

3) **Sexy characters**. Jordie and London Marriott were the eye-candy. Jaimee P. was the cute-but-accessible character.

4) **Dramatic conflict.** Characters need to fight each other, as well as a common enemy, in order to keep things interesting. Viewers like conflict. That's why I told the president the most powerful PR weapon he had was continuing to wage the most intense form of human conflict: war.

5) **The Winner(s).** All my shows—be it *The Assistant, the Bachelor* or *Survival*—end up with one person triumphing over the rest, someone who embodies all the best qualities that defines the American can-do spirit. And Saddam's capture was the ultimate challenge, a veritable Super Bowl of reality TV competition. Of course, unlike past shows I've done, we were rigging the show. The winner—the President—was pre-determined (in the interests of national security and the President's political survival).

6) **The Hook**. Call it a gimmick. Whatever you call it, it's the one thing that makes the show fresh and new. *The Bachelor* is about a single guy picking from a pool of women. *The Bachelorette's* hook is a woman picking from a pool of guys. *Who Wants to Marry My Dad*'s hook is that the kids are finding a new wife for their widowed dad. You get the picture.

7) **The Twist**. You need an unexpected plot twist to come out of nowhere at the end. A sterling example was in *Joe Millionaire*,

when the girls found that the guy they were vying for wasn't rich, and, in fact, was a construction worker who made like twenty-thousand a year.

I'm proud to say that, yes, I came up with the hook for *Who Wants To Be An American Hero*. And that hook was the paparazzi. They seemed fresh to me. I couldn't believe no other producer had thought of this. Maybe that's why I'm called a visionary. Heroes are a vital part of the American experience, and often times heroes come in unlikely forms.

There's a quote from writer Bernard Malamud that I tore out of a book many years ago and taped on my computer that reads, "Without heroes, we are all plain people, and don't know how far we can go." This idea is the inspiration for every show I do and *Who Wants To Be An American Hero* was supposed to be the ultimate expression of this ideal. Supposed to be.

The second I saw that picture of Saddam Hussein in *Them! Weekly*, I looked on the bright side. I realized that not only had Saddam been discovered, but he had been found by a celebrity photographer. The photo credit said the photographer was Jordie Black. And that's where I started my casting. But Jordie gave me a really good idea. By telling me how badly he wanted to break up Tom Peppers's marriage to his ex-girlfriend, he had given me an idea for a new character (Tom) and created some delightful conflict. I guess it just snowballed from there, and the story took off. It was a reality producer's dream.

As much as I like to take credit for things, I simply cannot take credit for the show's twist. Even a producer as brilliant as me couldn't have manufactured what was about to happen to the President's show. The best stuff is the unexpected stuff. You can't plan for disaster, but it is disaster that makes for the best train wreck television.

JORDIE BLACK

Photographer, Operation Hollywood

Did you really think I would join that snake Tom Peppers's team just because Bronco wanted me to and there was a lot of money to be made? No way, Jose. This was my chance to nab a piece of the fame that my pictures had created for so many idiot celebrities. Money is no longer our culture's most powerful tool; it's celebrity. And I wanted a taste of it. I know it sounds cheesy and cliché, but I really believed Mark was going to make me a star. Plus, yeah, it was a chance for me to show Kim—in front of a national TV audience—that I had all those qualities that I had lacked and Tom had. As an American hero, I would be rich, influential and, most important of all, famous. And I'd still be really good looking and a tiger in the sack. It was one of those can't-miss opportunities. To tell you the truth, I almost pulled it off ... until it got all fucked up.

MARK BURTON

Executive Producer, *Who Wants To Be An American Hero*

It occurred to me that not only were the paparazzi one of the last classes of professionals not to be featured on a network reality show, but they also were perhaps the most distinctly American. What group more symbolizes the Constitution in action than photographers breaking down the artifice of propaganda by snapping images of public people in real situations. I've always felt the paparazzi get a bad rap, that people like to blame them for being the purveyors of our culture's sick obsession with celebrity, when, in fact, they are only feeding the hunger already there. They are the ultimate service providers.

Like pornographers, paparazzi produce images that public desperately craves but desperately doesn't want to admit it craves. Our political leaders used to be the personification of American values. No more. As documentarians of human behavior, the paparazzi are the last remaining human symbols of truth, justice and the American way. And, selfishly as a TV producer, they were absolutely delicious.

Like I said before, casting—next to editing—is the single most important element of so-called reality television. *Survival* tapes for six weeks, but my producers and I spend six months traveling the country looking for the right characters. It's all about the right mix. That's what I was telling George from the start. It's all about the cast. You need the sexpot (London), the nerd (Barry Posner), the dumb jock (Arnold Schwarzenegger), the genius (Powell), the naif (Jaimee P.), the token black or Asian (Condi Rice), the arrogant SOB (Donald Rumsfeld/Colin Powell/Karl Rove/Condi Rice/Dick Cheney/George Tenet/George Bush), the gay guy, the ambitious one (Tom Peppers), the old fart (Bronco), the evil mother-fucker (Saddam), and the love-able idiot (George Bush). This was perhaps the most difficult show I've ever had to cast, yet also the most compelling.

Basically, it came down to this: I had two weeks to cast the single most important television show of my life. George wanted to wrap up production by the first of the year, and then have the show ready to air on Fox News Channel during the final months of the 2004 presidential campaign as counter-programming to

Michael Moore's propaganda film that we knew was coming out. The President was smart enough to know that, as he told me, "the best defense is a good offense." And George wanted to make sure he had an answer to that *Fahrenheit 9-11* film. He wanted to inspire the voters, to show them his leadership power and show off the American spirit in action by showing the underdog paparazzi—with no training, no language skills, just determination and guts—hunt down the world's most notorious celebrity.

MSNBC'S "HARDBALL WITH CHRIS MATTHEWS"

19 November 2003

CHRIS MATTHEWS: GOOD EVENING, AND WELCOME TO "HARDBALL." TONIGHT'S TOPIC: IS LONDON MARRIOTT THE NEW MONICA LEWINSKY? JOINING US IN THE DEBATE: IN NEW YORK, LEFT-WING SATIRIST AND ALL-AROUND KNOW-IT-ALL **AL FRANKEN**. VIA SATELLITE IN BOSTON IS M.I.T PROFESSOR AND FAMED LINGUISTICS SCHOLAR **NOAM CHOMSKY**. AND IN THE STUDIO WITH ME IS AUTHOR AND JOURNALIST **BOB WOODWARD**, AS WELL AS FORMER SPECIAL PROSECUTOR **KENNETH STARR**, WHO PROSECUTED BILL CLINTON IN THE LEWINSKY AFFAIR.

LET'S START WITH KEN STARR. DO YOU THINK THE PRESIDENT'S REALLY DOING LONDON MARRIOTT?

STARR: First of all, Chris, that's a question that I am reluctant to even validate with a response. The President is a very Christian man, with strong moral convictions, and I highly doubt that even a young, blonde, vivacious, promiscuous, luscious, lascivious and downright *sexy* young woman of London Marriott's caliber would make the President compromise his sound Christian values. It's a highly dubious proposition.

MATTHEWS: THAT'S BULL-COCKY, KEN, AND YOU KNOW IT! THAT GIRL'S SO SEXY SHE COULD COMPROMISE THE POPE! LONDON IS HOT, HOT, HOT! AND WHILE WE'RE AT IT, I SHOULD HAVE OUR PRODUCERS DO A HAND-CHECK ON YOU OVER THERE. YOU SEEMED A LITTLE TOO EXCITED WHILE TALKING ABOUT HER.

STARR: You are wrong, but you're entitled to your opinion.

MATTHEWS: DAMN RIGHT, I AM! THIS IS CHRIS MATTHEWS. YOU'RE PLAYING HARDBALL!

STARR: But while you are entitled to voice your opinions, why must you always SHOUT said opinions when we all can hear you perfectly clear?

MATTHEWS: I DON'T KNOW, KEN. MAYBE BECAUSE SHOUTING CREATES A SENSE OF URGENCY AND IMPORTANCE TO AN OTHERWISE IDIOTIC AND TRITE EXERCISE IN MASS COMMUNICATION. PLUS, HEY, IT'S GOOD FOR RATINGS.

AL FRANKEN: Uh, er, may I chime in here, fellas?

MATTHEWS: GO AHEAD, FRANKEN. YOU'RE NEXT UP ON "HARDBALL"!

FRANKEN: Did you ever notice that all conservatives are lying liars and all liberals always tell the truth and are all-around better human beings? And that Rush Limbaugh is a big fat idiot?

MATTHEWS: NO. I DIDN'T. AND GET A NEW DOGMA, AL. THAT SCHTICK IS GETTING STALE.

NEXT UP, BOBBY WOODWARD. SO, BOBBY, IS THE MEDIA PAYING TOO MUCH ATTENTION TO LONDON MARRIOTT AND NOT ENOUGH TO, SAY, THE FACT THAT WE INVADED IRAQ SEVEN MONTHS AGO AND SADDAM HUSSEIN STILL HAS NOT BEEN FOUND?

WOODWARD: Yes, I do believe that my colleagues in the media have let the White House somewhat off the hook in recent weeks. In fact, I have here in my hands a study released this week by the Freedom Forum. It finds that the amount of ink and broadcast time dedicated to Ms. Marriott's low-cut tops and length of her skirts has out-numbered by a three to one margin stories about the war in Iraq. For the Bush White House, I'd call this a victory, for it has effectively distracted the American public from the Achilles heel of this administration: the fact that we have not yet found any WMD's nor have we captured Saddam Hussein. It's brilliant media strategy. It's as if they've fashioned Clinton's fatal flaw—nubile young women — into their own life-saving propaganda. Bush is using the Bimbo Factor to his advantage. Absolutely brilliant strategy.

MATTHEWS: INTERESTING STUFF. THANKS, BOBBY. ... SO, PROFESSOR CHOMSKY, WHAT DO YOU MAKE OF ALL THIS MESS FROM YOUR PERCH UP IN THAT IVORY TOWER?

CHOMSKY: I believe the most important word I've heard thus far in this rather stimulating debate was one uttered by Mr. Woodward: propaganda. If one looks up "propaganda" in the dictionary one would see that it is defined as "any information or ideas methodically spread to promote or injure a cause, nation or other entity or enterprise." Another very relevant term was uttered by Mr. Franken: truth. Of course, truth is "information conforming with a fact or reality." I postulate that none of us on this panel, nor anyone in the viewing audience –

MATTHEWS: TWENTY SECONDS, PROFESSOR. WE'VE GOT TO GO TO COMMERCIAL.

CHOMSKY: Well, what I'd like to say is that we as a society no longer can differentiate between propaganda and truth, because the line between the two phenomena have so blurred. Particularly, in the world of contemporary politics, these terms have been rendered all but meaningless. I'd submit that we need to —

MATTHEWS: TEN SECONDS. MAKE IT SNAPPY.

CHOMSKY: Therefore, we need to create a new word to describe the most common form of information conveyed by our elected officials. And, if I may, I'd like announce here tonight the word I've created.

MATTHEWS: OK. FIVE SECONDS.

CHOMSKY: The word is Truthaganda. Chris, I contend that we are living in an age of Truthaganda.

MATTHEWS: PROFESSOR, I HAVE NO IDEA WHAT YOU JUST SAID. ... BUT NEXT UP ON "HARDBALL": A MAN WHO KNOWS HOW TO SPREAD PROPAGANDA BETTER THAN ANYONE ELSE—GUERILLA FILMMAKER MICHAEL MOORE. ... YOU'RE WATCHING "HARDBALL."

SADDAM HUSSEIN

Former President of Iraq

So I lay there in my room in the Venice Suites Hotel just off the boardwalk watching your stupid American television shows. Saddam could not believe what his eyes were seeing and what he hear. All this banter about things that don't really matter. Your country invaded another without provocation because why? Because I took a joke a little too far! I never had any weapons, and Hans Blix knew it, the U.N. knew it, and your Secretary Powell knew it. Too bad no one bothered to tell Mr. Bush that I never had any so-called "weapons of mass destruction." Honestly. Near the end there I was lucky if I could get Ali, my palace maintenance guy, to fetch me a firecracker. For Allah's sake!

Thousands of blessed Iraqi people were massacred in their homeland by the infidels, and, by the way, hundreds more Americans killed by brave Iraqi warriors. But I turned on your television and see you talking about another porn star working in the White House. In my country, it was a privilege for the president to sleep with porn stars. My boys Uday and Qusay (may Allah's light shine on them) took care of their father in that department. I don't understand all the—how do you say?—all the *fuss* about a president having sex. Saddam has had sex with many women, and it is a badge of honor. Saddam has no shame to his game.

But there you Americans sat, you have your president killing innocent Iraqi women and children, yet you focused on how Saddam, the supposed evil dictator, was on the loose and a danger when in fact your own president was the greatest danger to your sorry nation. Oh, how I enjoyed seeing the Americans play their expensive game of hide-and-seek as I tanned in L.A.!

Saddam likes to read. Saddam is well educated, a brilliant man. I've read about Josef Goebbels, the propaganda minister for the Nazi regime, who used to say that if you tell people big lies often enough they will eventually believe them. I'm not saying I haven't lied to my people; all leaders must lie at some point to persuade their public. But it was always for their own good when I lied. But George Bush's lies are only meant to glorify himself. They do nothing for his people. Splat! I spit on him and his father and their arrogant ways.

I know it may surprise some to learn that Saddam really did enjoy his time in America, despite it being led by vile men out to get Saddam. How did Saddam get to America, you ask? How did the Great One make it past the Americans' supposed top-notch security and land on their soil? Well, Saddam will tell you how he did it.

Before the stupid Americans even dropped a single bomb in their unjustified assault on the Iraqi people, I had already landed on their soil, hiding under their noses on the beach at Venice. It was easy. Saddam uses his mind. Saddam cannot be out-smarted. Saddam snuck into Jordan in the middle of the night on the eve of the bombing campaign. I knew the Americans would look everywhere but in their own back yard, so, with almost a million dollars in cash in my suitcase and a fake passport and disguise, I flew to Los Angeles. It was easier to do than taking over Kuwait. Ha-ha-ha-ha!

The Great One enjoyed his time in Los Angeles. I visited all the sights and, much to my surprise, made great friends—though Saddam was disappointed in the La Brea Tar Pits, which I had hoped would be bigger. And I found the homes of Beverly Hills to be nothing but shanties in comparison to my great palaces up and down the great fertile crescent between the Tigris and Euphrates. I've always been a big fan of American TV. One of my crowning of achievements was requiring that Iraqi television run re-runs of the *Charles in Charge* and the *Beverly Hillbillies*, my favorite shows of all time. So funny, Saddam thinks. By coincidence, one of the best friends I made on the Venice boardwalk was a man who play guitar and sing parodies of American TV show theme songs. His name was Rufus and he was quite plump. But, let Saddam tell you, Rufus had a good country-western voice. Merle Haggard good. Saddam's favorite song was his parody of the *Beverly Hillbillies*, which I have memorized and for you I will sing:

Come and listen to a story 'bout a man named Bush

His IQ was a zero and his head was up his tush

He used to drink like a fish and drive drunk all about

Lucky for him, his daddy would bail him out

DUI, that is ... Criminal record! Covered up.

The next thing you know bad-boy Bush goes to Yale
He could barely spell his name but the school wouldn't let him fail
He spent his college days drunk with his frat folk
And that's when we think he started to snort the coke
Blow, that is. White gold! Nose candy.

Then comes that stupid war in Vietnam
His parents say, Georgie, stay in Texas with dad and mom
Let the blacks and poors, they say, get blown up and scarred
Then we'll get you a spot in the Texas Air Guard
Bogus job, that is. Drinkin' with the boys. Draft dogder!

Some twenty years later, Georgie gets a little bored
So he runs for President, claiming Jesus is his Lord
He wins the race for Prez 'cuz the Jews couldn't punch the holes
That's why when the war went south so did his standing in the polls
Approval ratings, that is. Public opinion. Down the toilet!

Y'all vote him out, ya hear?

Saddam loves that Rufus! But he was just one of the reasons why the boardwalk at Venice became my home away from home for those many months I spent eluding Bush's stupid CIA. There, I became something of a local celebrity amid the homeless, the dancers, the magicians and the misfits who have been discarded by their callous fellow Americans. I was surprised to find very nice American tourists who would walk up to me on the boardwalk and, laughing, ask to have their picture taken with me, a man they thought was a look-alike of the Great One. If only America's war-mongering leaders were as friendly as their citizens. To be honest, Saddam felt more appreciated on that Venice boardwalk than he did at times as president of the great nation of Iraq.

In America, there is no greater royalty than Hollywood celebrities. I've learned that in America Tom Hanks is more beloved than George Bush—rightfully so, I might add. He was very good in *Forrest Gump* and *Saving Private Ryan. Bosum Buddies*, not so good. I never quite understood the power of your celebrities until I came to America and saw its magazines and its TV shows and saw that Hollywood celebrities wear the finest clothes and jewels and live in the most expensive mansions. They live like the Great One did in his homeland before the infidels raped its people. The Hollywood stars walk the red carpets and are revered by their fans. They are the American royalty, the true great ones of their nation as Saddam is the great one of his nation.

I got a taste of that royal treatment in Venice beach, embraced by total strangers who loved me for the sole and simple reason that I looked like someone famous. Imagine if they would have known it was the real Saddam! Never mind that I massacred, tortured and suppressed hundreds of thousands of my own people in a brutal reign of terror. Americans can forgive the famous for anything.

My time in America was not without some struggle, however. My hotel room was robbed in August, and they took all my money. But, again, being a Venice celebrity saved me from the poor house.

After I was robbed of my a hundred grand stash, I went down to the boardwalk and started charging ten bucks every time someone snapped their "Saddam Look-Alike" photo. I even developed a marketing technique, in which after the photo was taken I would ask them, "What's the greatest nation in the world." Assuming I wanted to hear Iraq, almost every time they would respond, "Iraq."

"No," I would say, extending my hand out palm up. "The greatest nation is Do-nation."

Don't ever let anyone tell you that Saddam doesn't have a sense of humor!

Capitalism is not bad; it's the capitalists who are the bad ones. They let greed get in the way of doing the right thing. Saddam always acted on behalf of the sovereign nation of Iraq, Saddam looked out for his people. Oil was the blood of my great nation, and I wanted everyone to drink from that cup, which is why I would open up my palaces to the common people every few years.

And I learned another very important and fascinating thing about this troubled nation of America. I learned that I had wasted the better part of twenty years trying to play games with American politicians. All along, Saddam should have been making friends with Hollywood celebrities, because it is through them that one can reach the hearts and minds of the American people.

So when the thugs, along with their black woman leader, broke into my hotel and arrested me in the middle of *Seinfeld* re-runs, and then put me on a military plane back to Iraq, I very soon knew what was in their feeble brains. I could read the black woman like the great Koran. She wanted to make George Bush a celebrity by making it look like he and his sad minions had captured the world's biggest celebrity! American leaders are so predictable. They are like children, fat and arrogant children. I spit on them. Blech!

But those leaders forgot the first tenet of war as once stated by your very own president Eisenhower: It's the size of the fight in the dog, not the size of the dog in the fight. This is why, no matter how many bombs they drop, no matter how many soldiers Bush sends over there, Saddam will prevail.

CONDOLEEZA RICE

National Security Adviser

Yes, I recognize that I may have exercised poor judgment in allowing the president to convince me to break the law in our implementation of Operation Hollywood. However, I always took actions that I believed were for the betterment of the United States and freedom-loving people all around the world.

And that includes my getting my hands dirty in the apprehension of the criminal himself in his hotel room. I had no choice. The risk of information about the operation leaking was too great to involve anyone else. It was risky enough that the two MP's with me learned of Saddam's whereabouts on our very soil.

I would regret not being totally candid with you about the details of the capture. It was shortly before midnight when the pistol-toting MP's broke down his hotel door, with me, dressed in black jeans and a black sweatshirt, on their heels. Mark Burton trailed behind us with a video camera, a' la *Cops*.

We had expected some sort of struggle, some level of resistance. Instead, what we found was a grandfatherly Middle Eastern man in boxers eating Pringles on his bed as he watched television. He was well-groomed, his mustache as expertly trimmed as it ever was, and he was tan and fit. He looked like he had been on the vacation of a lifetime. I was envious. I was the one who needed a vacation.

"Who are you?" Saddam asked us. "Why do you bother me?"

"No, sir," I replied. "The real question is, who are *you*?"

"I am the president of Iraq," he said defiantly. "I am the greatest leader of the greatest nation of the world. And I am on vacation. Go away! *Dharma and Greg* is about to start."

The MP's cuffed him, tied a bag over his head, and twenty-two hours later he was sitting in an isolation cell in the basement of the Abu Ghraib prison outside of Baghad, where for the next couple months he would lie waiting, on hold until Mark would tell us when to insert him into that spider hole south of Tikrit.

Admittedly, it was not my proudest moment as a public official. But it was imperative that the American people feel safe, that they believe that their public officials were protecting them in an increasingly unsafe and unpredictable world. If they were to find out that Saddam had been living among them for the last five months, there would be mass neuroses. The president did not want that, I did not want that, and, most of all, the American people would not have wanted that. As Mark Burton likes to say over and over again, "Give the audience what they want." And that's exactly what we did.

JAIMEE P.

Photographer, Operation Hollywood

I can't explain why I took a picture of Bronco in that horrific moment. I guess it's just second nature for me. While everyone cowered in the back of the truck, I just started snapping away at the chaos, at the raw agony on Bronco's face. Some might think that taking photos at a time of such great human tragedy is exploitative, but I think it's vital and beautiful. Nothing is more true than human drama. And, as a paparazzi, that's what I capture on a daily basis. Is the bloody image disgusting? You bet. Does it tell someone more about the reality of war than some lame, talking-head panel on a cable news channel? I crave to capture reality. As a photojournalist, it's not my job to worry about whether it is tasteful or proper. It's my job to capture it.

But the most important thing that taking that picture taught me is that you just have to go for everything in life. You can't stop and ponder. You must act. And you can't be afraid to fail. For how much I hate my sister Gwyneth for all her faux qualities, the one thing I have to respect is that even from an early age she knew what she wanted out of life.

The explosion, from which Tom protected me with his body, jarred loose the fear that had been stopping me from finding true love. It made me wake up to the fact that the man of my dreams was lying on top of me, protecting me, guarding me from danger. And I would get him.

MSNBC'S "HARDBALL WITH CHRIS MATTHEWS"

01 December 2003

MATTHEWS: NEXT UP ON "HARDBALL"!!! WAS PRESIDENT BUSH'S RECENT THANKSGIVING DAY VISIT TO TROOPS IN IRAQ A SHAMELESS POLITICAL PR STUNT? JOINING US TONIGHT: IN OUR STUDIO, SEXY WHITE HOUSE PRESS SECRETARY **LONDON MARRIOTT**. VIA SATELLITE FROM BAGHDAD, EGO-MANIACAL TV PERSONALITY **GERALDO RIVERA**. AND FROM HIS BRENTWOOD ESTATE, CALIFORNIA GOVERNOR **ARNOLD SCHWARZENNEGER**.

FIRST UP, LONDON. SO TELL ME, ARE YOU WEARING ANY UNDERWEAR?

LONDON: Of course not, Chris. Don't be silly.

ARNOLD: If I may butt in, I don't beleef her, Chris. Arnold vants her to prove she's really has nussing under her skirt.

LONDON: Shut up, Arnold. You've already seen what is under here anyway.

MATTHEWS: IS THAT THE TRUTH, ARNOLD? HAVE YOU REALLY SEEN MS. MARRIOTT'S KITTY KAT?

ARNOLD: Dis accusation is totally false, and I have to say it's such a shame that poleetics today is about tearing people down personally because you don't like their ideas.

LONDON: Uh, hello, Arnie! Like, my parents gave your campaign a million dollars. And, duh, like I am a Republican too.

MATTHEWS: YOU KIDS GOTTA GO GET A ROOM. NOW, BACK TO THE TOPIC AT HAND. GERALDO, WHAT WAS THE TOPIC AT HAND?

GERALDO: THE PRESIDENT'S BRIEF VISIT HERE WITH TROOPS LAST WEEK ON THANKSGIVING.

MATTHEWS: OH, THAT'S RIGHT. BUT, GERALDO, COULD YOU NOT SHOUT? I AM THE ONLY ONE ALLOWED TO SHOUT ON THIS SHOW!

GERALDO: How's this? Quiet enough for you, you egomaniac?

MATTHEWS: MUCH BETTER. PLEASE, CONTINUE.

GERALDO: Well, Chris, as I first reported exclusively on Fox News Channel before any other news outlet in the entire solar system, indeed the president did come visit some troops here in Baghdad. He served them food, shook hands, posed for pictures and gave an impromptu speech thanking the troops for their patriotism and sacrifice. It was quite moving and I witnessed it exclusively. And because I've become such a shill for the U.S. military, I was invited by the president to be the only journalist to witness Bush's visit with the troop. It was Bush's first visit to Iraq since the invasion eight months ago. And I was the only one there, a worldwide FOX NEWS exclusive. Chris?

MATTHEWS: GERALDO, DID YOU SAY THAT YOU ARE REPORTING THIS EXCLUSIVELY?

GERALDO: Yes, Chris, I was the only reporter on the ground able to witness the touching, historic visit to the –

MATTHEWS: I'M JUST PULLING YOUR CHORD, RIVERA. WE ALL GET IT. YOU THINK YOU ARE THE GREATEST REPORTER IN THE HISTORY OF TELEVISION WHEN YOU'RE REALLY JUST A FRAUD.

GERALDO: Thanks, Chris.

MATTHEWS: NOW, ARNOLD, BACK TO YOU. HELP ME UNDERSTAND SOMETHING. HOW LONG CAN PRESIDENT BUSH GO TRYING TO DISTRACT THE AMERICAN PUBLIC WITH THINGS LIKE DRAMATIC TROOP VISITS AND HOT BLOND AIDES IN MINI-SKIRTS? I MEAN, AT WHAT POINT IS THE AMERICAN PUBLIC GOING TO SEE THROUGH THE PROPAGANDA AND DEMAND A) SHOW US THE WEAPONS OF MASS DESTRUCTION AND B) FIND US SADDAM HUSSEIN.

ARNOLD: First of all, I have sources very close to da president who tells dese tings like how we are very close to finding Saddam. Maybe even closer than we thought. I sink that we will find him very soon. As for the so-called weapons of mass destruction, who needs them. The world already has The Terminator!

MATTHEWS: WHAT MAKES YOU SO SURE WE'LL FIND SADDAM?

ARNOLD: I am The Arnold, the Terminator, don't you forget dat. Arnold knows everyting. Just ask Maria!

LONDON: Oh, yeah? What a crock. You don't even know if I am wearing underwear!

ARNOLD: Oh, London, don't tempt me. You know if I was dere in the flesh and so forth that I would find out for myself.

LONDON: Is that a promise, big boy?

ARNOLD: As long as Maria doesn't find out it is. Hahahahaha.

MATTHEWS: ARNOLD, SINCE WHEN DOES MARIA CARE ABOUT YOUR PHILANDERING? I MEAN, HAVEN'T YOU ALREADY CHEATED ON HER WITH TWO HUNDRED WOMEN? I'D THINK SHE'D BE IMMUNE TO IT AT THIS POINT.

ARNOLD: Oh, I'm only kitting with you guys. In fact, I took some sexual harassment class and tings like dat and don't do such tings anymore. Ahnuld keeps it in his pants dese days.

MATTHEWS: WELL, ON THAT NOTE, WE HAVE TO GO. UP NEXT ON HARDBALL: COULD I BE ANY MORE LOUD AND ANNOYING? OUR PANEL WEIGHS IN.

TOM PEPPERS

Bureau Chief, Operation Hollywood

We started calling them Elvis sightings. In the month we had been inside Iraq we had over three-hundred Elvis sightings—that is, successful photographic captures of taxi cab drivers and passengers. From Baghad to Fallujah to Tikrit, we were able to surreptitiously fix our TinyShot™ cameras on the faces of possible Saddam loyalists that would lead us to Saddam. Instantly, our images were uplinked to a spy satellite and beamed to the eggheads back in Washington. According to Barry, who spent most of his time talking on the phone to the bozos back in D.C., none of the faces thus far had matched Saddam's or anyone in his innermost circle of sordid bastards who.

Bronco's injury had only increased our motivation. That's the pap character. Just ask any celeb who has been stupid enough to go ballistic on a photographer. When fucked with, we fuck back. Especially Jordie. After Bronco was flown back to the States to recuperate, Jordie was no longer the cocky surfer-dude with a chip on his shoulder. He acted like a mature man on a mission. And, as the team leader, it was a great thing to see. Barry kept calling it "the American spirit at work." And, I have to admit, I was starting to feel patriotic for the first time in my life. I started feeling like all my years of chasing around stars to get images had trained me for this important mission, and we had finally found our groove.

And then one day while Jaimee and I were walking the streets of Mosul pretending to be Canadian journalists interviewing taxi drivers with our translator Rashid, I suddenly had an epiphany: If Saddam were still alive, he wasn't in Mosul. Nor was he in Falloujah. Nor was he in Baghdad, for that matter. I'd like to say this brilliant thought came to me on my own. But that would have been the old Tom Peppers, the slimy celebrity magazine editor who used to take credit for everyone else's scoops. No, this one, I have to give all the credit to Rashid.

RASHID

Translator, Operation Hollywood

I was born in Iraq and grew up under the shadow of Saddam, under his intimidation and oppression. I saw firsthand the power that propaganda can have on the psyche of a nation. But I was among the lucky few who were able to get out and live in a free and open society where individuals can find their own personal truth: America.

A few months before the U.S. invasion of Iraq, I moved to Calabasas, California, to live with my grandparents and enroll at UCLA. Calabasas is about twenty miles up the 101 freeway from Hollywood, and home to a handful of celebrities who hide behind the planned city's gated communities, among them Rebecca Romijn and Jessica Simpson. Calabasas is also home to more Middle Easterners per capita than anywhere else in Southern California. It was in Calabasas than I got to see the celebrity world that I had only read about in the magazines that I had to beg, borrow and steal to see back in Iraq. I compare my personal discovery of celebrity - from watching Jessica shop at the Commons, to spying on Rebecca as she sipped Frappuccinos (no whipped crème)—to the feeling of falling in love. What attracted me most to the world of celebrity was that it the phenomenon is so distinctively American. But you all take it for granted. It is a privilege to worship your Hollywood celebrities. Back home, we were told who we could idolize, and it was almost always Saddam or his evil band of thugs. Celebrity obsession and worship is perhaps the single greatest expression of freedom in America. I mean, I guess voting is supposed to be, but who votes anymore?

So joining Operation Hollywood was something of a no-brainer for me because I knew it would not only put me in contact with the media who enable America's favorite pastime, but I just might become a celebrity myself. The hardest thing was pretending I didn't speak English well, plus lying to Tom and the gang. They are good people with good intentions, so I guess it makes me something of a hypocrite to have lied to them (like Saddam did to my people) for my own personal gain. I do feel shame about that. But Mark says that's the American way. On top of that, he promised to cast me on the next season of *Survival*!!!

TOM PEPPERS

Bureau Chief, Operation Hollywood

For weeks, if I wasn't snapping photos or in search of taxis, I was talking to Rashid. He had told me he was born and raised in Baghad, majored in English at the University of Baghdad and had even worked as an Arab translator for Saddam. He was a wealth of knowledge, but I always felt like something was not right about him at all. He almost seemed unusually more American than Iraqi. I just chalked it up to his watching too many *Full House* and *Joanie Loves Chachi* reruns.

On the ride back to the hotel one night, we started talking about the strict Iraqi social structure, and the intricate code of loyalty and silence that comes with it.

"The most important thing you have to understand if you are to understand an Iraqi is the tribal tradition," Rashid said in his thick accent. "Tribal loyalty comes before loyalty to country. Let me give example to you. Last month, I found out that a former classmate of mine had tipped off some U.S. soldiers on the whereabouts of two Shi'ite clan leaders. Two weeks later, those clan leaders were killed by the soldiers in a raid. What happened? The tribal leaders told my friend's father that he must kill his son, or the tribal leaders would kill him and his entire family. So the man shot his own son. It's ingrained in you that the tribe comes even before family."

I couldn't say I was surprised by this disturbing story. Spend a week in Iraq and you quickly realize that their culture is so different than ours that you can understand why the notion of the U.S. instilling American values there is a ridiculous enterprise. It would be like a group of Mormons coming to Hollywood and telling everyone that looks didn't matter, that it was the soul. That would go over about as well as Britney Spears in the New York Philharmonic.

But Rashid had given me the breakthrough I needed to find that evil needle Saddam in the giant haystack of Iraq. It occurred to me that Saddam had to be in and around Tikrit, his hometown an hour's drive north of Baghdad. I'd recently read that Saddam had grown up on a farm south of Tikrit, on the banks of the Tigris River. That is where he hid in 1959 after a failed coup attempt. In fact, Saddam had hid out on farms there, before swimming across the Tigris and fleeing to Syria.

In Hollywood, I had become well-versed in the art of war. And the first rule of combat is to know thy enemy. To break them, you have to understand how they think.

I asked Rashid, "So if a fellow member of your tribe knocks on your door and wants sanctuary what do you do?"

Rashid didn't hesitate. "You have to take them in. You have no choice."

The next morning we were on the road to Tikrit. I knew that if we didn't find him there, we would never find him.

BRONCO

Photographer, Operation Hollywood

I lost pretty much most of my right hand in the explosion. All my fingers were blown off. Interestingly, the only finger that I didn't lose was my index finger, a.k.a. my photo-snapping finger. Not that I would ever be able to hold a camera again.

I spent the first month after the accident high on morphine as the military surgeons at Bethesda Naval Hospital performed seven different surgeries on me: Two to remove shrapnel from my abdomen; four reconstructive surgeries on my mutilated hand; and one operation to install a cochlear implant in my right ear, which was rendered nearly deaf by the sound of the explosion, which happened just two feet from my ear.

You might find this hard to believe, but those weeks after the accident turned out to be the most enlightening of my life. I was nearing fifty years old and had just faced death right in the face. There's nothing like almost dying to make you feel so alive. I'd recommend it to everyone ... as long as they don't die.

Now that I had survived my near-death experience, I wasn't about to waste the final, at most, thirty years or so of my life. The good thing is that the explosion forced me to turn the page in my life, to end the chapter that was my life as a celebrity photographer. I needed to find a new calling. Luckily, as I lay in my hospital bed watching an E! *True Hollywood Story* on Nick Nolte, that new came calling to me in the form of a gray-haired guy named Ben. He wore a blue suit and the smile of a used Honda salesman.

BEN LAY

CEO, PALIBURTON INC.

We at Paliburton believe that American corporations have a civic responsibility that goes beyond merely making obscene piles of money. As the nation's largest provider of military equipment and services, Paliburton aims to reflect and uphold the old fashioned American values of patriotism, honor and sacrifice. At Paliburton, we put patriotism before profits. If it just so happens that being patriotic means making sure we have strong relationships with the Pentagon, the White House (we even have an ex-president, George H.W. Bush, on our board!) and every member of the Senate armed services committee so that we can secure multi-billion-dollar defense contracts, then, gosh darn it, we will do just that—and do it well.

With revenues of eighty-nine billion dollars last year alone, Paliburton, which employs over three-hundred thousand workers in forty-two different states and seventeen countries, is more than an engine of the American economy. We *are* the American economy! Our profits account for approximately thirty-eight percent of the nation's Gross Domestic Product. At Paliburton, we like to say we make more than just military weaponry and hardware. We make America work!

But in order to remain the world's biggest mega-corporation we must always strive to educate the American public. I know, I know. Cynics call it advertising, or public relations, or marketing. But we call it *education.* It's vital that Americans hear our message, that they know all the great things our technology does for people.

A perfect example of the Paliburton ethic is the CarefulBomb™. When the Pentagon came to us in the late 1980's and basically said, "We need smarter, more accurate bombs that limit collateral damage," we endeavored to find a solution.

After several years of research and testing, our engineers came up with a bomb that, through the use of state-of-the-art laser- and satellite-guided navigation systems, could obliterate the enemy within an accuracy of two millimeters. I am happy to report that since its implementation in the first Gulf War, the CarefulBomb™ has saved thousands of lives. Out of the 167,982 human beings who have been killed by a

CarefulBomb™, only 112 were innocent civilians. At Paliburton, we make weapons that save lives.

BRONCO

Photographer, Operation Hollywood

Maybe it was the ringing in my ears. Maybe it was the morphine drip. Maybe I feared that I wouldn't be able to take pictures anymore and had lost any ability to make money and needed to believe it was the right thing to do. Or maybe it was that I was stuck in my hospital bed like a cripple and bored of watching cable. Whatever it was, when I looked up and saw "Ben from Paliburton" standing at my bedside, it was as if an archangel had come for me—even if the guy was faker than Pamela Anderson's breasts and stiffer than a teenage boy at the Playboy mansion.

"Mr. Bronco?" the man said in a Texas drawl. He talked like a redneck but looked like a Wall Street banker. "You are Mr. Bronco, correct?"

"Just Bronco," I corrected him.

"Ok, Justin—"

"No, Bronco is my first and last name. My name's not Justin."

"Oh, please do accept my sincere apologies."

"Sir, don't sweat it," I replied in my morphine mumble. "As a man with one hand and shards of metal embedded in every part of his body, I'm just happy to be here."

"Well, that's just the kind of can-do spirit we are looking for!" the guy enthused. "We need more men like y'all."

"We?"

"Yes," he said. "We is Paliburton Inc. I'm Ben Lay, CEO of Paliburton. I'd like to welcome y'all into our family."

RONALD STUMP

Business Mogul/Reality TV star

I told Bush and Burton that they needed to find some corporate synergy for his Hollywood operation. It's not just a buzz word. It's the backbone of American business today. There's no sin in synergy, my friend. A great example is on my reality show, *The Assistant.* The young Ronald wannabes work for all my Stump enterprises, they drink Stump water, they fly in the Stump jet, they live in Stump tower, they gamble in Stump's casino, and, let's not forget, they star on Stump's television show. Let me tell you something they're not gonna tell you in business school: If you don't employ synergy, you are an idiot.

Speaking of idiots, I had no interest in helping George Bush solve his Saddam problem. I have enough problems just getting my hair not to look like a helmet, let alone deal with Bush's inability to think for himself. But let's face the facts here, people. I could do a better job running the country than that moron. I mean, every business Bush ever owned he mismanaged and ruined. I, on the other hand, know how to run a successful organization, and I know how to get things done. Listen here, pal: I know hot dog vendors on Coney Island who have more brains than this nitwit. If I had my way I would walk into the Oval Office, point my finger at Bush and tell him, "You're fired!"

But I won't do that because of Mark Burton. Mark is not only the executive producer of *The Assistant*, but he's also a good friend of mine. And I am loyal to my friends. I like to help those who help me. It's not only the right thing to do, but it's good business. So when Mark came to my office begging for advice on how to pay for this covert Operation Hollywood or whatever the hell they called it, how could I not offer him some?

"The President wants me to produce a reality show about the capture of Saddam Hussein, but we have zero budget to do it," he explained. "The Pentagon can't pay for it because it's so top secret."

I would have invested in it. But let's face it: I have enough money. I simply saw no upside. Plus, I didn't have a financial stake in that damn show. I mean, I had nothing in terms of back-end! So I just said, "Look, Mark. You need a corporate sponsor. Get a corporate sponsor that makes sense. Find a company that could benefit from being associated with this kind of para-military operation. Find the synergy, and make it happen." Now, listen to me. Some egghead business consultant would have charged Mark a hundred grand to give that kind of quality advice, but, being a good friend, I gave it to him for free.

Now, I'm a real estate guy. I don't know the first thing about this hunting-for-dictator crap. I could probably figure out that line of business in a day or two—if I wanted. But I don't care to do that. Since I'm an extremely busy man, I couldn't just sit around and bullshit all day with Mark, so I stood up to show him the door and added, "Tell that idiot Bush to tap Paliburton. A) It's run by a Texas redneck like him and B) They're the Republican National Committee's single biggest corporate donor. And they're coming out with a new, state-of-the-art camera. You could probably sell Paliburton on the product-placement opportunities alone."

I don't tell you this story to boost my ego. My ego is big enough. Just ask my ex-wives! But in case you haven't figured it out, what I am trying to tell you is that I am responsible for the TinyShot™ revolution. I tell you all this not because I want money or that I want Paliburton Inc. to lease office space in one of my buildings (though they have since become my biggest tenant in Stump Tower); I just want credit for coming up with yet another brilliant business idea.

GEORGE W. BUSH

President of the United States

I didn't like it that I owed Arnie a favor for putting me in touch with Mark Burton. Nor was I happy about that snake Ronald Stump coming up with the Paliburton camera tie-in. But, heck, I sure as hell loved what was takin' shape over there in Iraq by way of the *big idea*. We had compiled over a thousand hours of footage from the TinyShot™ video and still cameras that the paparazzi were carrying. Not too shabby, my friend.

On top of that, Paliburton had agreed to cover the budget of the show, which was thirty million bucks. Of course, twenty-five of it was to pay the paparazzi their reward money for "finding" Saddam; the rest covered basic production costs and whatnot. My friends at Paliburton were set to be some seriously happy campers. I had promised Benny Boy that when the show began airing (and viewers saw their American heroes using the cutting-edge imaging technology) they could transfer the military TinyShot™ into consumer use. Thirty mill wasn't going to be a bad investment for them. They expected to sell ten million units at a per-unit price of five-hundred bucks. For those of you countin' at home, that would total about five billion dollars in revenues. So it was a win-win for everyone. A win for corporate America. A win for the American people. A win for the paparazzi. A win for myself. Well, I guess that would make it a win-win-win-win-win situation.

Only problem is that none of my advisers—except for Condi—knew the big picture. Only me and Mark. It was time to let everyone in on the operation.

Like I said before, until that point I had to keep the information compartmentalized, on a need-to-know basis. Just like in those spy movies, you know. Plus, if word of what I was up to ever got back to my daddy he wouldn't like it at all. With his buddies Colin and Dickie and Rummy in my cabinet, it was always a risk that Daddy would find out. But it was time to let them in on the operation. I had ta do it, had ta bite the bullet. Bushie had no choice. I needed to bring my team together. After all, I am a uniter, not a divider.

BARRY POSNER

Special Assistant to the President

I was never the same person the instant I looked back at Bronco staring at the space where his hands once were. As blood drained from Bronco's arms onto the floor of the Humvee, as his teammates ran to his aid and frantically tried to stop the bleeding, as our soldiers opened fire and mowed down the teenage Iraqi who threw the IED into the truck, I could no longer put the interests of the United States before the interests of greater humanity.

I know it sounds radical that a career CIA officer such as myself could change his perspective so quickly. But I did. I had hired Bronco and the others to do a job; I was responsible for them. Sure, they knew the risks, and they had decided the chance to make six million dollars a piece was worth it. But it was my idea for all of us to drive into the heart of Baghad in a military vehicle. I should have known better. All I can say is, thank God that Bronco survived. Had he not, I couldn't have lived with myself for getting him in this situation.

I'd always prided myself as being a patriot in the war on terror. But when you see senseless death and injury occur before your very eyes, you begin to question the morality of your nation's effort. Going into it, I had my doubts about the president's ability to lead, about our mission in Iraq. And I let Dr. Rice, who was back in the SIT room, know it when I phoned her with the news of the explosion and the tragedy of Bronco's hands getting blown off.

"Is anyone else injured?" she asked.

"No, thankfully."

"So the objective of our mission is not in jeopardy, we still have the other three," she said coldly.

I couldn't take it any more.

"All of us nearly got our heads blown off and I all you care about is whether we'll still be able to find Hussein? Frankly, Dr. Rice, I expected more out of you."

"Listen, Mr. Posner. You're out of line."

"No," I shouted back. "You're out of line. And while I'm at it, how about this: You and the president's so-called liberation of Iraq is a total fiasco. We don't control the streets, they do." "They" being, in this case, a fifteen-year-old wearing a "Fuck Da Police!" t-shirt who was able to run up to our vehicle and hurl a bomb.

"That's the reality of urban warfare, and this was taken into account when we crafted our broader policy goals " she schooled me. But I would have none of it.

"Don't wonk me, Dr. Rice. If we're going to win this war on terror, we have to do more than capture a bad guy. We also have to construct something good. So let's say we get Saddam. Then what? Who do we replace him with? Maybe you haven't watched CNN lately, but the reality here is that most of them don't want a democratic Iraq. To them, democracy has resulted in more violence, more unemployment, more uncertainty. Democracy is not living with foreign soldiers pointing weapons at you and your family."

Dr. Rice didn't say a word. All that I could hear for ten seconds was the crackle of the satellite phone line. She knew I was right. I could hear her whispering to someone in the background. Finally, she said, "Hold on. The President wants to speak with you."

"Barry!" Bush said with frat-boy glee. "Heard about the accident. Sorry 'bout that. You're a hero, Barry. Glad you're doin' okay."

Just when I was about to ruin my career by telling the president he was a Grade-A asshole, he added, "But I heard the good news: Tommy boy might know where Saddam's hidin'. And if that's case, and you guys do find him, there is a certain job waiting for you back on the ranch."

"Yes, sir," I said, suddenly recalling why I embarked on this mission in the first place: to take over Dr. Rice's job when Bush promoted her to Colin's job. "I am very much looking forward to that, Mr. President."

"Good. Now go get 'em!" As I was about to hang up, the President added. "And one more thing: Now make sure everyone's usin' those TinyShot™."

Not knowing that I was merely a pawn in their propaganda game, I naively replied, "Will do, sir."

TOM PEPPERS

Bureau Chief, Operation Hollywood

Poor Barry. He really believed in what he was doing. He believed in all that duty-honor-country and hard-work-pays-off crap. He was the genuine article. The poor bastard had no clue the whole operation was a sham and that Jordie was in on it. And no way was I about to tell Barry or Jaimee just yet. Especially Jaimee. Jaimee wanted to believe she was doing something important, something self-less, something more meaningful than celebrity photography. Truth is, I wanted to believe that too.

It was hard not to tell anyone, and hard not to just go and confront Jordie and Rashid about their obvious collusion in the thing. I mean, it got to the point where Jordie was practically acting as a field producer and Rashid as his cameraman. Rashid was *supposedly* our translator and was *supposedly* shooting video only for surveillance purposes, but it became clear to me—but apparently not to anyone else—that something other than searching for Saddam was actually going on when Jordie started ordering Rashid re-shoot different things. Like down in Falloujah one day, Jordie snapped at Rashid after he didn't include Jordie in a shot of Jordie photographing seven taxi drivers sitting on an apartment balcony. "Jordie, who the fuck cares if he got you in the shot?" I confronted him afterward. "We're here to photograph *them*, not us."

"Well, maybe I'm tired of it being about them all the time!" he said.

I could tell by the way Rashid winced that the two were in cahoots. Initially, I figured they were shooting some sort of documentary. Mind you, at the time I had no clue that the conspiracy involved more than the two of them, that all of us were merely actors in this ill-conceived propaganda drama, puppets whose strings were being pulled by Bush.

Still, I didn't say anything. This was despite the fact that journalists are the worst secret-keepers. Most of us get into journalism because, at our core, we like to tell people what we know. So the fact that I had this news and wasn't sharing it was a serious departure from the norm for me. But Iraq had changed me so much I was no longer sure what my norm was any more.

I've never been one for touchy-feely, Hallmark moments. I mean, in my line of work you have to turn off the emotions and just focus on the work. If I stopped for one second to consider that all the prying I did into stars' personal lives could hurt them I wouldn't be able to do the job, like if a soldier considered that an enemy also had a family who loved him back home. That being said, I was totally caught off guard by what happened on the road to Tikrit.

We were all sitting in the van - Jaimee, Jordie, Barry, Rashid and me—and we were exhausted in that totally spent way only the 110-degree desert heat can wipe you out. Combine that kind of heat with all the drama of the last few weeks—from the daily emotional roller coaster of the Elvis sightings, to the tragedy of seeing Bronco almost die—and your emotions tend to bubble to the surface.

As we sped to the farming village nine miles south of Tikrit where Rashid suggested Saddam could be hiding, I felt that our mission, which began as a quest to nab our respective pieces of that twenty-five million dollar reward, had opened my eyes to a whole new world outside of Hollywood. And I'm not just saying this because we weren't just papping another beautiful idiot in Beverly Hills. No, this trip was getting to my heart, a place I hadn't let anyone touch since I fell in love with psycho Jessica a few years earlier.

The sun had just set over the sandy horizon to our left as Jaimee, who was crammed next to me in the van, rested her head on my shoulder. Two months under the desert sun had turned her skin a sexy reddish-brown hue, and the less-than-tasty Iraqi food had caused her to drop about ten pounds from her five-foot-six frame.

Most eye-catching, however, was her hair. Jaimee always had brown hair, and I just assumed it was her natural color, since no woman in Hollywood dyes her hair brown. But Jaimee is not your typical L.A. chick. Her hair had grown out blonde over the last few weeks. Now, it's not exactly a big secret that I'm a sucker for blondes. They turn me into emotional mincemeat. You might say blondes are the kryptonite to my Superman. But my secret weapon is that blondes are also the spinach to my Popeye.

Suddenly, Jaimee no longer looked like the slightly off-kilter, obsessive, workaholic photographer. As she nestled onto my shoulder and I began stroking her tousled, sandy-blonde hair, I realized there was no other woman in the world whom I felt more comfortable with and closer to than Jaimee. Not only did I realize that I loved her, but I realized that I had always loved her, from the first time she came to my office to show me her stalkerazzi photos. But, until now, I never had sexual feelings for her. Man, I had a real awakening in that van: I was in love.

A good journalist also has to be a good judge of character. You've got to be. A journalist is constantly being fed information from different sources who have differing agendas, and somewhere between the source and their agenda is the real story, the truth. And I sensed Rashid's character flaw from the get-go. I always sensed that something wasn't right, from the way he seemed so unlike any other Iraqis to his intense knowledge of American magazines and celebrities. I mean, he knew that ICM wasn't a kind of missile but rather a Hollywood talent agency. But what really gave it away was that the earpiece he wore was not, as he told us, playing music from his iPod. Rather, every now and then I could hear a voice of someone who sounded like they were coaching him what to say. Rashid was an actor—and not a very good one. I'd been around Hollywood scumbags enough to know a rat when I smelled one. You can't fool the fooler.

But I didn't have the heart to tell Jaimee or Barry, who obviously didn't even realize what was happening. For all his faults, one great quality that Barry has is that he's a bad liar. But I knew we were being set up, being watched. And our own cameras were doing the watching. Of course, if it had been my idea I would have thought it was fucking brilliant. But since it wasn't, I wanted to ruin it for the bastards.

WHITE HOUSE SITUATION ROOM

11 December 2003

2:13 p.m.

Attendees: President Bush, Colin Powell, Dick Cheney, Karl Rove, Condoleezza Rice, Tom Ridge, Donald Rumsfeld, George Tenet, London Marriott, Ben Lay and Mark Burton

BUSH: Glad y'all could make it today for this very important meeting. Dickie, good to see you got some color in your face for change. Karl, put down the muffin. London, you look absolutely stunning today.

MARRIOTT: Why thank you, Mr. President. So do you.

BUSH: So, moving on ... Rather than go through the usual hoopla, I might as well cut right to the chase. It's time that all of you—my inner *sanctuary*—knew a little bit about ...

RICE: Sir, you mean *sanctum.*

BUSH: Sanctum, sanctuary ... you guys know what the hell I mean. As I was sayin', I wanted to alert everyone in this room to a top-secret mission we've been conducting over the last few months that, in just two days, will copulate in the —

RICE: Sir, uh, you mean *culminate*, right?

BUSH: Condi, please, can't ya see I am tryin' to govern here! Like I was sayin', in just two days from now we will capture Saddam Hussein.

(Everyone erupts in spontaneous applause; Bush beams.)

BUSH: Yes, good news indeed. But there's a little twist to it, my loyal friends. He will be discovered by a group of celebrity tabloid journalists whom I have handpicked for this operation. The final moments of the capture will be videotaped by cameras that we've had following these folks for the last couple months over there in Iraq. Look up there. (Bush points to the flat screen monitor showing a live streaming video of the team speeding up the highway to Tikrit.)

We dubbed this here mission Operation Hollywood. The producer of this show is none other than Mark Burton; he's the fella right over here and he is privately funded by my boys down at Paliburton, which of course is run by my pal Ben, who's sitting right next to Mark.

Now, mark, could you come up here and give London, Condi and the boys a briefing? I'm gonna run out and get a PB&J sandwich real quick. Hey, anyone want a sandwich? Huh? Anyone? Fine then. Okey dokey. I'll be right back. Go ahead, Mark.

BURTON: Thanks, George. Good afternoon, everyone. I want to start off by saying I love all of your work, which we've been documenting with hidden cameras for the last several months. We will be handing out release forms at the end of the meeting. Don't worry, you guys really know how to put on a good show. London, I have to say hats off for an especially wonderful job handling the press. You're going to be a star some day. And, Dick, thanks for letting me take over your office for the last few weeks; I know it sucks to lose your window office. You were probably wondering why you were booted. Well, now you know!

We have had more than enough drama going on the behind the scenes over the last few weeks, and I apologize on behalf of Dr. Rice and the president that you all have not been briefed on the production. Secrecy is paramount in the TV world, what with so many broadcast and cable networks trying to steal everyone else's show ideas. You understand.

That accidental and highly unfortunate explosion suffered by our cast member was the perfect example of why I call it "unscripted" television. No one told that Iraqi kid to toss the bomb into the back of the Humvee. You couldn't write something as dramatic as that. I mean, just as our heroes—real American heroes—were embarking on their mission, then that kid goes and—kaboom!—injects a tragedy into our story. It was the most dramatic plot point in the history of reality television. I'm talking more dramatic than when Richard Sacks got naked on *Survival*! Not only was it damn good TV, but it gave us a perfect conclusion to Act Two. And now I am here to report that it is time to move the story forward into Act Three. It is time for resolution.

Thanks to the generous support of Paliburton, our principal performers will be paid what they believe is reward money for finding Saddam. And I am happy to announce that Paliburton has selected as its new spokesman Bronco, a man who embodies the American values that Paliburton stands for.

(Bush returns to the SIT room eating a sandwich.)

RUMSFELD: Mr. President, what is this jack-ass mouthing off about? I can't understand a god damn word he's saying? Have you all lost your freakin' minds?

BUSH: Listen, Rummy, Mark-o is explainin' how we're gonna capture Saddam Hussein. Just listen for a sec will ya? Go on, Mark-o.

BURTON: Thanks, George. The weekly magazine sales have been indicating that the public is once again starting to think more about the war in Iraq, and, despite a wonderful performance by Ms. Marriott, they aren't being effectively distracted by her media appearances.

Fortunately, the timing is perfect. Our cast is ready to start Act Three, in which Saddam Hussein will finally be captured by our rag-tag team of patriotic tabloid journalists, which I will be joining tomorrow on a sheep farm nine miles south of Tikrit. It should be quite a reveal, as we call it in the business.

RUMSFELD: Wait one second here, cowboy. What's all this bull-cocky about a "cast" and a "show"? I'm not understanding this.

RICE: Donald, we have been videotaping the operation with the intention of airing the hunt as a reality series on network television.

POWELL: This all sounds like the most absurd idea to come out of this administration, and there have been some real doozies—that whole Weapons of Mass Destruction fiasco notwithstanding. Not to mention that even as the secretary of state I had no idea about this covert paramilitary operation. Just another example of you all trying to keep me out of the loop on matters of national interest. I am personally offended, and, as an American, appalled at your recklessness, including the president's.

MARRIOTT: Chill out, sugar. Seriously, it's not, like, a big deal. TV is all that matters anymore. And Mark will make sure we all get residuals, I'm sure. We will make money off this right, Mark?

BURTON: Yes, everyone in this room will share in the profits of the show. Certainly. There is a back end.

RUMSFELD: Well, Mr. President, you and this La.La Land fairy can kiss my back end! I have to respectfully submit that this is, at best, unorthodox, and, at worst, grounds for presidential impeachment proceddings. And the last thing I want is for Dick to take over—no offense, Dick.

CHENEY: Buzz off, bifocals!

RUMSFELD: What I am trying to say is that this is just plain wrong.

ROVE: But, everyone, you must think about the much-needed euphoria and patriotism that will sweep the nation when they learn of Saddam's capture. The president will skyrocket back up in the polls, the economy will kick back in, and the American people will once again have faith in their great nation. Right, Mr. President?

BUSH: Mark?

BURTON: Exactly.

RUMSFELD: But let me get this straight. You are trying to tell me these tabloid folks are going to be able to do a job that our own highly trained military professionals haven't? I find that hard to believe.

BURTON: I have to defer to the president on this question. Sir, would you like to explain how we really found Saddam?

BUSH: Well, heck, I guess I do have some explainin' ta do ... but, more important, we have a mission to accomplish here. It's time to (Bush fashions air quotes with his fingers) capture that bugger Saddam.

PHONE CONVERSATION

ARNOLD SCHWARZENNEGER AND GEORGE BUSH SENIOR

12 December 2003

7:14 p.m.

ARNOLD: Mr. Bush, it is Ah-nuld. How are you, sir?

BUSH SR.: Doin' good. Just watchin' *Wheel of Fortune* here in the livin' room. I wish all the best to you and Maria.

ARNOLD: Tanks. And how is that old firecracker, Mrs. Bush, doing dese days?

BUSH SR.: Who, Bar?

ARNOLD: Yes.

BUSH SR.: Oh, she's *ready to die.*

ARNOLD: What is dis you say to Ah-nuld? Pleece, say it ain't so.

BUSH SR.: Just givin' you the old Dana Carvey impersonation of me. Just kiddin' with ya. Pulling your proverbial leg. Gotcha!

ARNOLD: Oh, Mr. Bush, you are funny man with dese tings you say and so forth, but I have something serious to discuss wit you today.

BUSH SR.: I am all ears, as Ross Perot might say. Heck. Well, anyway ...

ARNOLD: I am calling about your son.

BUSH SR.: Oh, yeah, my boy. Doin' a great job, isn't he? Love that Dubya.

ARNOLD: No, actually, Ah-nuld doesn't tink so. He must stop someting immediately, and I need your help.

BUSH SR.: Anything for you, Arnold. You know that. No stronger bond than that between two Republicans, after all.

ARNOLD: Well, I have made zee mistake of giving him some crazy idea to make a reality show with dis guy Mark Burton.

BUSH SR.: Love his shows! Barbara and I never miss an episode of *Survival.* Love it, I'll tell ya. Heck. It's good stuff.

ARNOLD: His shows are fine. The problem Ah-nuld has is that dis Burton guy has arranged an elaborate hoax in which da paparazzi photographers with their cameras and tings like dat will find Saddam Hussein. It's called Operation Hollywood, or some sing like dat. But I cannot let his happen, sir, because I am against dese paparazzi nowadays, working on pushing legislation and tings through Congress. I am working on dis Save Our Actors movement, this effort to prevent my famous friends from being hounded by the paparazzi and tings. Look, Mr. Bush, dese celebrities are like the big oil companies were for you: They are my base. I need to make them happy, and if I make them happy then someday I will have the money to save your silly Republican party and become president of the United States.

This is Ah-nuld's cause, my mahk to make on politics. Plus, I get to work with dis Gwyneth Paltrow girl. She's got quite the nice body, which Ah-nuld like very much and so forth. You know, maybe I can score some points with her and get in her political pants.

BUSH SR.: Let's stay focused here, Arnold. These are very serious allegations you are making about my boy, and I want to make sure that I am understanding this correctly. You're saying my boy is not being honest with the American people? You are telling me he's engaging fraudulent activity? If true, well, then that's just unacceptable. I will have to bring my boy to task.

ARNOLD: Unfortunately, yes, he is doing dese tings, Mr. Bush. It stahted when he called me asking if I knew any Hollywood guy who could help him with dis situation of having found that Saddam was living on a beach in Calee-fornia. Some magazine found Saddam living on the beach or some sing like dat. And, you know this London Marriott girl is all part of it too, Mr. Bush. He is making some sort of reality show and so forth and wanted a hot blonde for ratings and tings like dat. But the White House is not Hollywood, I beleef. So, pleece, he must be stopped, Mr. Bush.

BUSH SR.: Arnold, you can count on me to take care of this. That damn boy of mine, always getting in trouble. Embarrassing us, is what he's doing.

ARNOLD: Tank you so much, sir. Ah-nuld appreciates your help.

BUSH SR.: All the best, Arnold.

PHONE CONVERSATION

PRESIDENT BUSH AND GEORGE BUSH SENIOR

12 December 2003

7:31 p.m.

PRESIDENT BUSH: Y'ello.

BUSH SR.: Dubya, it's your father speaking.

PRESIDENT BUSH: Daddy! What can I do for ya?

BUSH SR.: Well, Dubya, for starters, you can stop acting like a nitwit.

PRESIDENT BUSH: What do ya mean, Daddy? I'm doin' the best job I can for the American people, protecting our global interests, takin' care of the domestic front, tryin' to build a coalition of freedom-loving peoples around the world. And, heck, I'm about to find Saddam for ya! I just wanna please ya, Daddy.

BUSH SR.: Listen, Dubya, I know you're doing the best you can, but your mother and I are worried that you might be taking this whole Saddam thing a little too far just because you want to please me. Getting that evil dictator is important, but upholding the laws of this great nation are more important. You understanding me, son.

(silence)

BUSH SR.: Dubya. You still there?

PRESIDENT BUSH: Wait a sec, daddy. *Access Hollywood* is doin' a behind-the-scenes piece on me and London in the White House. Let me watch the end of it.

BUSH SR.: Turn that crap off! This is just the reason why I am calling you. Pardon me for saying this, son, but you've got your head up straight up Hollywood's ass!

PRESIDENT BUSH: Sorry, Daddy. I am really sorry.

BUSH SR.: Just because most politicians are starting to look and behave more like entertainers and less like leaders doesn't mean you have to do the same. You need to stay true to your roots, son. Hollywood governs the land of fantasy; we Bushes govern the land of reality.

PRESIDENT BUSH: You are right. The critics are right. I am the shrub to your bush.

BUSH SR.: Listen here, Dubya. You have to put a stop to this silly reality TV show—immediately. I cannot allow you to do this Saddam show. You are disgracing yourself and the family, not to mention your country.

PRESIDENT BUSH: Who told you about the show? It was Dick wasn't it?

BUSH SR.: No.

PRESIDENT BUSH: Then it had to be Powell.

BUSH SR.: Wasn't him, either. I just got a phone call from Arnold, and he told me all about it.

PRESIDENT BUSH: Aw, man. I knew I couldn't trust a guy who wears makeup!

BUSH SR.: Well, son, you should be more concerned with making sure the American people can trust *you*. If any word ever got out that you staged Saddam's capture, that you had used this show as some sort of propaganda tool, well, then you would just be crucified by the Democrats. You understand what I am saying?

PRESIDENT BUSH: Yes, I do. I have sinned. But I only did it because I wanted you to be proud of me. Saddam tried to kill you, Daddy. Don't forget that. He wanted to bomb you when you visited Kuwait. Heck, Daddy, his staying in power was probably the biggest reason why you didn't get re-elected. I just wanted to restore your honor and dignity. I love ya, Daddy.

BUSH SR.: I love you too, Dubya. But listen to me: I told you when you got the job that there would be a lot of distractions, that there'd be temptations to do the wrong thing. Look what it did to that idiot Clinton. This whole celebrity thing is a mirage. It looks tasty and attractive, but it's not real. It's not politics. It's not what our founding fathers envisioned the presidency to be about. Luckily, you have a chance to do the right thing. Now, stop lollygagging and go and do it.

PRESIDENT BUSH: Okay, I will. But, please, don't tell Mama about this. Please don't.

BUSH SR.: As long as you stop this, I will not tell her. She'd fly off the handle. Now you go, son. Make an executive decision. If you need me, I'll be right here in the living room with your mom watching *According to Jim.*

PRESIDENT BUSH: But, Daddy, might you change your mind if I told you something.

BUSH SR.: Can't imagine what you could tell me, but go ahead.

PRESIDENT BUSH: Well, your company is in on this show. And I'm talking financially. They can profit.

BUSH SR.: Paliburton?

PRESIDENT BUSH: Yessir. They're the corporate sponsors of the mission, which, in a history-makin' move, will be broadcast on all four of the major TV networks startin' a month after the capture. And Paliburton's TinyShot™ is the official camera of the show. Sort of like how Coke sponsors *American Idol.* But our show is called *Who Wants to be An American Hero.* Paliburton thinks they can sell over ten million cameras just through the publicity of the show. Not bad, eh?

BUSH SR.: Interesting son. Very interesting. Now you are speaking my language. Corporate kickbacks is something of a family tradition!

PRESIDENT BUSH: I just want to make ya happy, Daddy. And I know there's nothing that makes you happier than a fat wallet for our friends. So ya think you just might change your mind and let me pull off this here operation?

BUSH SR.: Well, I have to admit, you've got a great deal going on there. Something very vital, very American about this TV show. And, as I've always said, a good leader is open to new ideas, open to changing his mind.

PRESIDENT BUSH: So do I have your blessing?

BUSH SR.: Son, all I can say is to ask the Lord in prayer and then do what you think is right for the country.

PRESIDENT BUSH: I will, Daddy. Tell Mama I love her.

BUSH SR.: I will, son. But before I go I feel compelled to share something with you. You know that your mom and I have always felt that your brother Jeb was more presidential, and I know that's been hard for you to deal with over the years. And I know I've come down on you real hard for golfing too much and starting wars for dubious reasons and for generally being an all-around goof. But, Dubya, you've really earned my respect with this plan. You've got nothing to prove to me. I'm already proud of ya.

PRESIDENT BUSH: Thanks, Daddy.

BUSH SR.: One more thing, though.

PRESIDENT BUSH: What's that?

BUSH SR.: Son, don't screw this one up.

MARK BURTON

Executive Producer, *Who Wants To Be An American Hero*

Right after the President revealed Operation Hollywood to his cabinet I flew overnight to Iraq to field-produce the finale. Too much work had been put in to leave anything to chance.

First of all, there were still too many story lines that needed resolution. Would Barry get his promotion? Would the president be deemed a hero or a buffoon? Would Tom realize his goal of fame fortune and patriotic glory? Would Jaimee P. win Tom's heart? Would Jordie get his fame and win Jessica back? Would Bronco survive (I kept him hidden in the hospital the whole time to build the drama and suspense)? Most important of all, would this band of Americans finally find Saddam? I do not think I was overstating when I believes this would be the greatest finale in the history of reality television!

We'd spent months building up the suspense, and all the dramatic tension had afflicted me with a case of producer's blue balls. And, thanks to that sneaky little shit Tom Peppers, my producing balls are still aching. He really fucked things up.

JORDIE BLACK

Photographer, Operation Hollywood

The plan was working perfectly. I was convinced that Barry, Jaimee, and Tom had no clue what was going on, that they really thought the advice from Rashid that we head to the village of Adwar was the real deal.

The day before we were to capture Saddam, Burton had parked an orange taxi next to two mud huts on a sheep farm a few hundred yards from the Tigris. The plan was that Tom and the rest of us would see the taxi and appropriately stake out the farm, waiting in the bushes with their cameras fixed on target. Bush and Rice and the rest of the skeptical cabinet watched the entire scene play out on a satellite hookup, as Burton coached Rashid and the Saddam handlers through their earpieces.

As instructed, just after sundown the two Iraqi informants posing respectively as Saddam's cook and driver forced Saddam at gunpoint to walk out the hut and climb into the nearby "spider hole" that a couple production assistants had dug. Tom, Jaimee and I were crouched fifty yards away in different parts of the field, snapping dozens of frames, instantly uploading the images back to Langley. Rashid, meanwhile, videotaped the entire thing with an infrared TinyShot™ camera. I could just see Jessica watching all this play out. Jessica, the girl who loves sex and celebrity. Jessica, the girl who knows I am good at sex, and would now see that I was the breakout star on *Who Wants To Be An American Hero*. Jessica, I prayed, would want me back when this was all over.

The plan was to ambush the farmhouse the following morning, on a Sunday. Burton wanted to make sure the light was good, and morning was the best for it. Luckily, Tom agreed with me. So we went back to our base camp on the banks of the Tigris a couple miles away and went to sleep.

When I woke up on what was supposed to be D-Day, Tom's and Jaimee's tents were gone, and they were nowhere to be found. So I walked over to Barry's tent and found that he also was missing. Only Rashid, who lay snoring in his tent, remained at our camp. Something was wrong, but I didn't know exactly what it was until I woke Rashid and we drove to the farmhouse. Outside, the orange taxi was gone and the property looked abandoned. When I stepped inside the house, nothing was inside. None of the furniture, clothing and stacks of American dollar bills Burton had planted there. It was totally bare! Panicking, I ran out to the spider hole that Mark Burton's guys had dug in the ground, the pit that was supposed to contain Saddam Hussein. It too was empty.

"Oh, no," Rashid moaned, handing me his Sidekick. "This cannot be true! For Allah's sake!"

He had called up an A.P. news report on his screen. "Jordie," he said. "You must read this story."

Sunday, December 14, 2003

TIKRIT, Iraq (A.P.)—*Eight months after the fall of Baghdad, U.S. soldiers found and captured former Iraqi dictator Saddam Hussein in a hole in the ground late Saturday night nine miles south of his hometown of Tikrit. Saddam was taken into custody without a single shot being fired. At a news conference in Baghad earlier today, coalition civil administrator L. Paul Bremer brought Iraqi journalists to their feet with shouts of joy when he announced, "Ladies and gentleman, we got him!"*

In a scene right out of a Hollywood movie, about 600 soldiers of the Army's 1st Brigade, 4th Infantry Division, and special operations forces of Task Force 121 conducted the raid in the farm in the village of Ad Dawr. Troops converged on a two-room mud hut that lay between two farmhouses. One room, which appeared to sere as a bedroom, was in disarray with clothes strewn about the area. The other room was a crude kitchen. Armed with a pistol, Saddam was found lying disoriented in 6-foot-deep hole equipped with a basic ventilation system. Military video released to the media shows a group of coalition soldiers patting each other on the back in celebration outside the compound.

U.S. officials said they had received "actionable intelligence" from someone close to Saddam's inner circle that he was hiding out at the location. The operation was dubbed "Red Dawn."

"It just takes finding the right person who will give you a good idea where he might be, and that's what happened," said Lt. Gen. Ricardo Sanchez, commander of U.S. forces in Iraq, who in recent weeks had received intelligence that narrowed the search to the Tikrit area. "The Iraqi people no longer need to fear a return of Saddam's tyranny," President George W. Bush said in a televised speech to the nation. "We should all be proud of the nation's military and intelligence professionals. Their dedication in bringing this brutal dictator to justice has led to today's victory for peace and democracy."

U.S. officials, citing classified informants, would not reveal the identities of the tipsters who led forces to Saddam's hideout other than to say it was three Americans inside Iraq who would receive the $25 million reward that had been offered to anyone with information leading directly to Saddam's capture.

TOM PEPPERS

Bureau Chief, Operation Hollywood

Once I figured out that Operation Hollywood was a fraud, there was no way I could go through with the capture. It was too false, too antithetical to the values that I try to uphold as a journalist. I embarked on it to do something patriotic, but deceiving the American people seemed like the most unpatriotic thing I could ever do.

So after everyone dozed off at the base camp on that Saturday evening, I woke Barry and Jaimee and told them what I really thought was going on.

Predictably, Barry didn't believe me at first. "Peppers, you can't be serious," he said. "Do you really think the president would go to all this trouble just to stage Saddam's capture? Prove it."

When I went through the list of obvious signs that it was a sham, he finally agreed. "Peppers," he said. "I have to hand it to you. You can smell a dirt bag from a million miles away."

"Takes one to know one," I joked.

Jaimee, however, was not at all surprised to find out that Jordie had tried to pull a fast one on us. Jamie, after all, trusts no one.

Nonetheless, we all decided it made most sense to tip off the true American heroes, the members of the U.S. military who, for the last nine months, had been trying in earnest to find Saddam. That's when Barry, Jaimee and I drove up to U.S. headquarters in Tikrit and informed General Odierno, commander of the Army's 4th Infantry Division, the exact whereabouts of Saddam. In exchange for the information, the Army brass promised to give us the $25 million bounty on Saddam's head.

But I didn't do it for the money. I didn't do it for love. I didn't even do it to rain on Bush's parade and Paliburton's plan for world domination. And I didn't even do it because I wanted to mess with Jordie. (Though I'd be lying if I didn't admit all these things were motivating factors.)

Truly, I shut down the operation for two reasons.

For one, journalists like me are supposed to cover the people behind the stories, not become the stories. This seems like a quaint idea in a media age of ego-centric blowhards like Bill O'Reilly, Geraldo Rivera and Michael Moore. But it's an idea—objective disinterest—that my professors at Columbia Journalism School were right about. As a celebrity journalist, I might report and photograph what some may think is superficial information on superficial people. But at the end of the day at least I know that what I have reported to the American public is true—something the president cannot say. And I have no doubt I did the right thing. Euphoria swept across Iraq as most citizens, besides the minority insurgents, once and for all felt free of Saddam's brutal regime. The U.S. military experienced a much-needed morale boost. And, perhaps most satisfying of all, since Who Wants to be an American Hero never made it to air, Jordie never won Jessica back.

Following Saddam's capture, Jaimee and I returned to *Them!* and have kept working. We have invested most of our reward money in the TinyShot™ IPO, as the technology is quickly becoming the industry standard and revolutionized the world of paparazzi. You think celebrities are photographed every minute of every day? Just wait until every kid in town is carrying TinyShot™. I'm not thrilled that Paliburton is getting rich too. But I guess you have to pick your battles. The rest of our reward money—about a million bucks of it—we have spent on fighting Gwyneth Paltrow's absurd Save Our Actors movement.

As for Barry Posner, Bush fired him for disobeying his orders and ruining Operation Hollywood. So I hired him as*Them!*'s news director and he now uses the world-class intelligence gathering skills he learned while with the CIA to cover the world of celebrity, infiltrating the camps of Hollywood's biggest stars, and in so doing has helped us break more exclusive stories than ever before. How do you think we got the exclusive pictures of the J. Lo wedding?

Plus, Barry is making five times more money and finally getting laid on a regular basis—by, believe it or not, London Marriott, who, after she left the White House, fell in love with him after seeing Barry on all those satellite feeds beamed back to the White House from Iraq. I have already warned him to look out for hidden cameras.

I'm not interested in exposing Bush and his propaganda plan. History is good to those who are honest; it's the deceivers who suffer. Bush will have his day of reckoning. Lying and not revealing the truth are two different things, and by not ratting out Bush and his cronies I chose not to reveal the truth. But then Mr. Baker came asking these questions and, as a fellow journalist, I felt compelled to answer them.

But I maintain that America want to believe their president is a good person. In our political leaders and our celebrities we see idealized versions of ourselves. And, at the end of the day, we want to believe we are all good people. Which brings me to the second and most important reason I arranged for the military—not a band of paparazzi—to capture Saddam Hussein: In Hollywood, we like happy endings.

For the latest news on Hollywood Hussein go to www.kenbaker.net.